Pansy

Ruth Erskine's Crosses

Pansy

Ruth Erskine's Crosses

ISBN/EAN: 9783337255084

Printed in Europe, USA, Canada, Australia, Japan

Cover: Foto ©Lupo / pixelio.de

More available books at **www.hansebooks.com**

"He has made everything beautiful in his time." p. 112.

RUTH ERSKINE'S CROSSES

BY

PANSY

Author of "Ester Ried," "Julia Ried," "Four Girls at Chautauqua," "Chautauqua Girls at Home," etc.

BOSTON
LOTHROP PUBLISHING COMPANY

PANSY
Trade-Mark Registered June 4, 1895.

CONTENTS.

	PAGE.
CHAPTER I.	
HER CROSS SEEMS HEAVY	7
CHAPTER II.	
SIDE ISSUES	24
CHAPTER III.	
A CROSS OF LEAD	40
CHAPTER IV.	
BITTER HERBS	56
CHAPTER V.	
SEEKING HELP	72
CHAPTER VI.	
FROM DIFFERENT STANDPOINTS	88
CHAPTER VII.	
ONE DROP OF OIL	104
CHAPTER VIII.	
FINDING ONE'S CALLING	121

	Page.
CHAPTER IX.	
A SOCIETY CROSS	136
CHAPTER X.	
OTHER PEOPLE'S CROSSES	151
CHAPTER XI.	
A NEWLY-SHAPED CROSS	167
CHAPTER XII.	
THE CROSS OF HELPLESSNESS	182
CHAPTER XIII.	
LOOKING FOR AN EASY YOKE	197
CHAPTER XIV.	
"THROUGH A GLASS DARKLY"	212
CHAPTER XV.	
RESTS	227
CHAPTER XVI.	
SHADOWED JOYS	243
CHAPTER XVII.	
DUTY'S BURDEN	258
CHAPTER XVIII.	
EMBARRASSMENT AND MERRIMENT	274
CHAPTER XIX.	
MY DAUGHTERS	290

CHAPTER XX.
A SISTER NEEDED 306

CHAPTER XXI.
TRYING QUESTIONS 321

CHAPTER XXII.
"THAT WHICH SATISFIETH NOT" . . 337

CHAPTER XXIII.
WHEREFORE? 350

CHAPTER XXIV.
"HEARKEN UNTO ME" 364

CHAPTER XXV.
"BITTER-SWEET" 379

CHAPTER XXVI.
"THESE BE THY GODS" 393

CHAPTER XXVII.
THE BAPTISM OF SUFFERING . . . 408

CHAPTER XXVIII.
"THE OIL OF JOY" 420

RUTH ERSKINE'S CROSSES.

CHAPTER I.

HER CROSS SEEMS HEAVY.

SHE stood in the hall, waiting. She heard the thud of trunks and valises on the pavement outside. She heard her father's voice giving orders to driver and porter. She wondered why she did not step forward and open the door. How would other girls greet their mothers? She tried to think. Some of them she had seen — school-girls, with whom she had gone home, in her earlier life, who were wont to rush into their mother's arms, and, with broken exclamations of delight, smother her with kisses

How strange it would be if she should do any such thing as that! She did not know how to welcome a mother! How should she? She had never learned.

Then there was that other one, almost harder to meet than a mother; because her father, after all, had the most responsibility about the mother; it was really his place to look after her needs and her comfort. But this sister would naturally look to her for exclusive attention. A sister! She, Ruth Erskine, with a grown-up sister, only a few years younger than herself! And yet one whom she had not only never seen, but, until the other day, of whose existence she had never heard! How perfectly unnatural it all was!

Oh, if father had only, *only* done differently! This cry she had groaned out from the depths of her soul a hundred times, during the two weeks of the father's absence. After she had turned away from the useless wail, "Oh, that all this had never been!" and resolutely resolved not to be weak and worthless, and desert her father in his need, and give herself up to vain regrets, she found that the regretting only took another form. Since it was, and must be, and could not honorably be gotten away from, why had he not faced the necessity long ago, when she was a child? Why had they not grown up together, feeling and understanding that they were sisters, and owed to each other a sister's forbearance?—she could not bring herself to say *love*. If her father had only settled it years and years ago, and brought the woman home, and made her position assured; and if the people had long and long ago settled down to understanding it all, what a blessed thing it would have been! Over and over, in various forms, had this argument been held with Ruth and her rebellious heart, and it had not helped her. It served to make her heart throb wildly, as she stood there waiting. It served to make the few minutes that she waited seem to her like avenging hours. It served to make her feel that her lot was fearfully, exceptionally, hopelessly hard.

There had been daughters before, who were called on to meet new mothers. Yes, but this was an old, old mother — so old that, in the nature of things, she ought, years ago, to have been reconciled to the event, and to have accepted it as a matter of course. But what daughter, before this, had been called upon suddenly to greet, and to receive in social equality an own sister? The more she thought of it, the more unnerved she felt.

And so the door was opened at last by Judge Erskine himself. His daughter had decreed that no servant should be in attendance. She wanted as few lookers-on as possible.

"Well, daughter," he said; and, even in that swift moment, she wondered if he ever spoke that quiet-toned, "well, daughter," to that other one. Then she did come forward and hold out her hand, and receive her father's lingering kiss. Something in that, and in the look of his eyes, as he put her back from him, and gazed for an instant into hers, steadied her pulses, and made her turn with a welcome to the strangers. There was an almost pleading look in those eyes of his.

"How do you do?" she said, simply, and not coldly; and she held out her hand to the small, faded-looking woman, who shrank back, and seemed bewildered, if not frightened. "Do you feel very tired with the long journey?"

"Susan," said her father, to the third figure, who was still over by the door, engaged in counting the shawl-straps and satchels. "This is my daughter Ruth."

There was an air of ownership about this sentence, which was infinitely helpful to Ruth. What if he had said, "This is your sister Ruth?" She gave her hand. A cold hand it was, and she felt it tremble; but, even in that supreme moment, she noticed that Susan's hair was what, in outspoken language, would be called red; and that she was taller than accorded with grace, and her wrap, falling back from its confinings, showed her dress to be short-waisted, and otherwise ill-fitting. Long afterward Ruth smiled, as she thought of taking in such details at such a moment.

It transpired that there was still another stranger awaiting introduction — a gentleman, tall and grave, and with keen gray eyes, that seemed looking through this family group, and drawing conclusions.

"My daughter, Judge Burnham." This was Judge Erskine's manner of introduction. For the time, at least, he ignored the fact that he had any other daughter. Very little attention did the daughter bestow on Judge Burnham; eyes and wits were on the alert elsewhere. Here were these new people to be gotten to their rooms, and then gotten down again; and there was that awful supper-table to endure! She gave herself to the business of planning an exit.

"Father, you want to go directly to your rooms, I suppose? I have rung for Thomas, to attend to Judge Burnham, and I will do the honors of the house for Susan."

Very carefully trained were face and tone. Beyond a certain curious poise of head, which those who knew her understood betokened a strong pressure of self-control, there was nothing unusual. Really, the worst for her was to come. If she could but have made herself feel that to send a servant with this new sister would be the proper thing to do, it would have been so much easier. But for the watchful eyes and commenting tongue of that same servant she would have done it. But she sternly resolved that everything which, to the servant's eyes, would look like formality, or like hospitality extended simply to guests, should be dispensed with. It would do to ring for Thomas, to attend Judge Burnham; but a daughter of the house must have no other escort than herself. On the way up-stairs she wondered what she should say when the room door closed on them both. Here, in the hall, it was only necessary to ask which satchel should go up immediately, and which trunk went to which room. But, when all the business was settled, what then?

She began the minute the attending servant deposited the satchels, and departed:

"Do you need to make any change in dress before tea, and can I assist you in any way?"

For answer, the young girl thus addressed turned toward her earnest gray eyes — eyes that were full of some strong feeling that she was holding back — and said, with eager, heartful tones:

"I am just as sorry for you as I can be. If there is any way in which I can help to make the cross less heavy, I wish you would tell me what it is."

Now, this was the last sentence that Ruth Erskine had expected to hear. She had studied over possible conversations, and schooled herself to almost every form, but not this.

"What do you mean?" she asked, returning

he earnest gaze with one full of bewilderment.

"Why, I mean that I have some dim conception of how hard, how *awfully* hard all this is! Two strangers to come into your home and claim, not the attention accorded to guests, but the position belonging to home! It is dreadful! I have felt so sorry for you, and for myself, all day, that I could not keep the tears from my eyes. I want to make myself as endurable as possible. If you will only show me how I will try very hard."

What was Ruth Erskine to reply to this? It *was* hard; she felt too truthful to disclaim it. Just now it seemed to her almost impossible to endure it. She tried to turn it off lightly.

"Oh, we shall live through it," she said, and the attempt to make her voice unconstrained startled even herself. Susan abated not one whit the earnestness in her voice.

"I know we shall," she said. "Because it must be done — because it is right — and because we each have an Almighty Helper. I asked your father, and mine, as soon as ever I saw him, whether you were a Christian. It seemed to me it would be an impossible ordeal if you were not. He *is* my father, Ruth. I know it is hard for you to hear me use that name, which you have supposed for so many years belonged exclusively to you. If it had been right, I could almost have made myself promise never to use it. But it wouldn't be the right way to manage, I am sure. Ruth, you and I shall both breathe freer, and understand each other better, if we admit from the first, that father has done wrong in this thing. Now I know that is dreadful to say. But remember, he is my father. I am not to blame because he loved your mother better than he ever could mine. I am not to blame for a bit of the tragedy any more than you are. And I have been a sufferer, just as you are. All my life I have been without a father's love and care. All my life I have had to imagine what the name 'father' must mean. I am not blaming him; I am simply looking at facts. We shall do better to face this thing. I really had something to forgive. He admitted it. I have forgiven him utterly, and my heart just bleeds for him and for you. But then we shall, as you say, get through all the embarrassments, and come off conquerors in the end."

Utter silence on Ruth's part. How shall I confess to you that this conversation disappointed and angered her? She was nerved to bear heavy crosses. If this new sister had been arrogant, or cringing, or insufferably rude and exacting, I think Ruth would have borne it well. But this simple, quiet facing of difficulties like a general — this grave announcement that she, too, had been a sufferer — even the steady tone in which she pronounced that word "father," gave Ruth a shiver of horror. The worst of it was — yes, the very *worst* of it was — this girl had spoken truth. She *was* a sufferer, and through no fault of her own, through Judge Erskine's pride and self-will. Here was the sting — it was her father's fault — this father who had been one of her strongest sources of pride during all her proud days of life. "It is true enough," she told herself, bitterly. "But she need not have spoken it — I don't want to hear it." And then she turned away and went out of the room — went down-stairs, and paused in the hall again, resting her arm on that chair and trying to still the tumult in her angry heart.

As for the sister, looking after her with sad eyes, she turned the key on her at last, and then went over to the great, beautiful bed — more beautiful than any on which she had ever slept — and bowed before it on her knees. What if Ruth Erskine had had to contend with a sister who never got down on her knees! Yet she positively did not think of that. It seemed to her that nothing could make the cross more bitter than it was. She opened the door at last, quietly enough, and went forward to where her father was standing, waiting for her, or for some one — *something* to come to him and help him in his bewilderment. He looked ten years older than when she saw him two weeks ago, and there was that appealing glance in his eyes that touched his daughter. A moment before she had felt bitter toward him. It was gone now.

"I brought Judge Burnham home with me," he said, speaking quickly, as if to forestall any words from her. "He is an old friend. He was a pet of your mother's, Ruth, in his boyhood, and he knew all about her, and about —— this.

I thought it would be better than to be quite alone at first."

"Yes," Ruth said, in a tone that might be assenting, or it might simply be answering. In her heart she did not believe that it would be better for them to have Judge Burnham in their family circle, and she wished him away. Was not the ordeal hard enough without having an outsider to look on and comment?

"When will you be ready for supper?" she asked, and, though she tried to make her voice sound naturally, she knew it was cold and hard.

"Why, as soon as Judge Burnham and —— they come down," he said, hesitatingly. What were they all going to call each other? Should he say "your mother," or should he say "Mrs. Erskine?" He could not tell which of the two seemed most objectionable to him, so he concluded to make that foolish compromise and say "they."

"Where did you leave Susan?" he questioned.

"In her room."

Ruth's tone was colder than before. Judge Erskine essayed to help her

"She is the only alleviating drop in this bitter cup," he said, looking anxiously at Ruth for an assuring word. "It has been a comfort to me to think that she seemed kind and thoughtful, and in every way disposed to do right. She will be a comfort to you, I hope, daughter."

Poor Ruth! If her father had said, "She is perfectly unendurable to me; you must contrive in some way that I shall not have to see her or hear her name," it would have been an absolute relief to his daughter's hard-strained, quivering nerves. It was almost like an insult to have him talk about her being a help and a comfort! She turned from him abruptly, and felt the relief which the opening door and the entrance of Judge Burnham gave.

The supper-bell pealed its summons through the house, and Judge Erskine went in search of his wife; but Ruth called Irish Kate to "tell Miss Erskine that tea was ready," flushing to the roots of her hair over the name "Miss Erskine," and feeling vexed and mortified when she found that Judge Burnham's grave eyes were on her. Mrs. Erskine was a dumpy little woman, who wore a breakfast-shawl of bright blue and dingy brown shades, over a green dress, the green being of the shade that fought, not only with the wearer's complexion, but with the blue of the breakfast-shawl. The whole effect was simply dreadful! Ruth, looking at it, and at her, taking her in mentally from head to foot, shuddered visibly. What a contrast to the grandeur of the man beside her! And yet, what a pitiful thing human nature was, that it could be so affected by adverse shades of blue and green, meeting on a sallow skin! Before the tea was concluded, it transpired that there were worse things than ill-fitting blues and greens. Mrs. Judge Erskine murdered the most common phrases of the king's English! She said, "Susan and me was dreadful tired!" And she said, "There was enough for him and I!" She even said his'n and your'n, those most detestable of all provincialisms!

And Ruth Erskine sat opposite her, and realized that this woman must be introduced into society as Mrs. Judge Erskine, her father's wife! There had been an awkward pause about the getting seated at the table. Ruth had held back in doubt and confusion, and Mrs. Erskine had

not seemed to know what her proper place
should be; and Judge Erskine had said, in pleading tone: "Daughter, take your old place, this
evening." And then Ruth had gone forward,
with burning cheeks, and taken the seat opposite
her father, as usual, leaving Mrs. Erskine to sit
at his right, where she had arranged her own
sitting. And this circumstance, added to all the
others, had held her thoughts captive, so that
she heard not a word of her father's low, reverent blessing. Perhaps, if she had heard, it might
have helped her through the horrors of that
evening. There was one thing that helped her.
It was the pallor of her father's face. She almost
forgot herself and her own embarrassment in trying to realize the misery of his position. Her
voice took a gentle, filial tone when she addressed
him, that, if she had but known it, was like
drops of oil poured on the inflamed wounds
which bled in his heart.

Altogether, that evening stood out in Ruth
Erskine's memory, years afterward, as the most
trying one of her life. There came days that
were more serious in their results — days that
left deeper scars — days of solemn sorrow, and

bold, outspoken trouble. But for troubles, so petty that they irritated by their very smallness, while still they stung, this evening held foremost rank.

"I wonder," she said, in inward irritation, as she watched Mrs. Erskine's awkward transit across the room, on her father's arm, and observed that her dress was too short for grace, and too low in the neck, and hung in swinging plaits in front — "I wonder if there are no dressmakers where they came from?" And then her lip curled in indignation with herself to think that such petty details should intrude upon her now. Another thing utterly dismayed her. She had thought so much about this evening, she had prayed so earnestly, she had almost expected to sail high above it, serene and safe, and do honor to the religion which she professed by the quietness of her surrender of home and happiness; for it truly seemed to her that she was surrendering both. But it was apparent to herself that she had failed, that she had dishonored her profession. And when this dreadful evening was finally over, she shut the door on the outer world with a groan, as she said, aloud and bitterly:

"Oh, I don't know anything to prevent our home from being a place of perfect torment! Poor father! and poor me!"

If she could have heard Judge Burnham's comment, made aloud also, in the privacy of his room, it might still have helped her.

"That girl has it in her power to make riot and ruin of this ill-assorted household, or to bring peace out of it all. I wonder which she will do?"

And yet, both Judge Burnham and Ruth Erskine were mistaken.

CHAPTER II.

SIDE ISSUES.

HOW did they ever get into such a dreadful snarl as this, anyway?

It was Eurie Mitchel who asked this question. She had seated her guests — Flossy Shipley and Marion Wilbur — in the two chairs her small sleeping-room contained, and then curled herself, boarding-school fashion, on the foot of her bed. To be sure it is against the rule, at this present time, for girls in boarding-schools to make sofas of their beds. So I have no doubt it was, when Eurie was a school-girl; nevertheless, she did it.

"Where should I sit?" she asked her mother,

one day, when that good lady remonstrated. "On the floor?"

And her mother, looking around the room, and noting the scarcity of chairs, and remembering that there were none to spare from any other portion of the scantily-furnished house, said, "Sure enough!" and laughed off the manifest poverty revealed in the answer, instead of sighing over it. And Eurie went on, making a comfortable seat of her bed, whenever occasion required.

On this particular evening they had been discussing affairs at the Erskine mansion, and Eurie had broken in with her exclamation, and waited for Marion to answer.

"Why," said Marion, "I know very little about it. There are all sorts of stories in town, just as is always the case; but you needn't believe any of them; there is not enough truth sprinkled in to save them. Ruth says her father married at a time when he was weak, both in body and mind — just getting up from a long and very serious illness, during which this woman had nursed him with patience and skill, and, the doctors said, saved his life. He discovered, in some way — I don't know whether she told him so or not, but somehow he made the discovery — that she lost possession of her heart during the process, and that he had gotten it, without any such intention on his part, and, in a fit of gratitude, he married her in haste, and repented at leisure."

"How perfectly absurd!" said Eurie, in indignation. "The idea that he had no way of showing his gratitude but by standing up with her, and assenting to half a dozen solemn statements, none of which were true, and making promises that he couldn't keep! I have no patience with that sort of thing."

"Well, but," said Flossy, coming in with gentle tone and alleviating words, just as she always did come into the talk of these two. "The woman was a poor, friendless girl then, living a dreadful boarding-house life, entirely dependent on her needle for her daily bread. Think how sorry he must have been for her!"

Eurie's lip curled.

"He might have been as sorry for me as he pleased, and I dare say I shouldn't have cared if he had expressed his sorrow in dollars and cents; but to go and marry me, promise to love and cherish, and all that sort of thing, and not to mean a word of it, was simply awful."

"Have you been studying the marriage service lately?" Marion asked, with a light laugh and a vivid blush. "You seem strangely familiar with it."

"Why, I have heard it several times in my life," Eurie answered, quickly, her cheeks answering the other's blushes. "And I must say it seems to me a ceremony not to be trifled with."

"Oh, I think so too!" Flossy said, in great seriousness and sweet earnestness. "But what I mean is, Judge Erskine, of course, did not realize what he was promising. It was only a little after Ruth's mother died, you know, and he — well, I think he could not have known what he was about."

"I should think not!" said Eurie. "And then to deliberately desert her afterward! living a lie all these years! I must say I think Judge Erskine has behaved as badly as a man could."

"No," said Marion; "he has repented. He might have gone on with his lie to the end of

life, and she would have made no sign, it seems
The *woman* can keep a promise, whether he can
or not. But think what it must have cost him
to have told all this to Ruth! Why, I would
rather tell my faults to the President than to
Ruth Erskine! Oh, I think he has shown that
there is nobility in his nature, and sincerity in
his recent profession. It would have been so
easy to have consoled his conscience with the
plea that it was too late to make amends. Still,
I confess I think as you do, Eurie. Marriage is
a very solemn covenant — not to be entered into
lightly, I should think; and, when its vows are
taken, they are to be lived by. I don't feel very
gracious toward Judge Erskine."

"Still, if the Lord Jesus and his own daughter can forgive him, I think we ought to be able to do so."

It was Flossy's voice again — low and quiet, but with that curious suggestion of power behind it that Flossy's voice had taken of late. It served to quiet the two girls for a minute, then Marion said:

"Flossy Shipley, I'm not sure but you have our share of *brains*, as well as heart. To be sure, in one sense it is none of our business. I don't believe he cares much whether we ever forgive him or not. But I believe I shall, and feel sorry for him, too. What a precious muddle he has made of life! How are they ever going to endure that woman?"

"Is she so very dreadful?"

This was Eurie's insinuating question.

"Father and Nellis called, but I could not bring myself to go with them. I was sure I shouldn't know what to say to Ruth. I tried to have them describe her, but father said she must be seen to be appreciated, and Nell would do nothing but shrug his shoulders and whistle."

"She is simply terrible!" Marion said, with emphasis. "I didn't stay fifteen minutes, and I heard more bad grammar and bad taste in the use of language than I hear in school in a week. And her style of dressing is — well," said Marion, pausing to consider a strong way of putting it — "is enough, I should think, to drive Ruth Erskine wild. You know I am not remarkable for nervousness in that direction, and not supposed to be posted as to styles; but really, it would try my sense of the fitness of things considerably to have to tolerate such combinations as she gets up. Then she is fussy and garrulous and ignorant, and, in every way, disagreeable. I really don't know how I am ever to —"

And at that point Marion Wilbur suddenly stopped.

"What about the daughter?" Eurie asked.

"Well," said Marion, "I hardly know; she impresses you strangely. She is homely; that is, at first sight you would consider her very homely indeed; red hair — though why that shouldn't be as much the orthodox color as brown, is a matter of fashion I presume — but she is large featured, and angular, and has the air and bearing that would be called exceedingly plain; for all that, there is something very interesting about her; I studied her for half an hour, and couldn't decide what it was. It isn't her smile, for she was extremely grave, hardly smiled at all. And I'm not sure that it is her conversation — I dare say that might be called commonplace — but I came away having a feeling of respect for her, a sort of feeling that I couldn't define, and couldn't get away from."

"Nellis liked her," said Eurie. "He was quite decided in his opinion; said she was worth a dozen frippery girls with banged hair, and trains, and all that sort of thing, but he couldn't give a definite reason, any more than you can, why he 'approved of' her, as he called it."

"I don't know what her tastes can be," continued Marion. "She doesn't play at all, she told me, and she doesn't sing, nor daub in paints; that is one comfort for Ruth; she won't have to endure the piano, nor help hang mussy-looking pictures in 'true lights'—whatever lights they may be. But I should imagine she read some things that were worth reading. She didn't parade her knowledge, however, if she has any. In short, she is a mystery, rather; I should like you to see her."

"Perhaps she is fond of fancy-work," suggested Flossy, somewhat timidly; whereupon Marion laughed.

"I don't fancy you are to find a kindred spirit in that direction, my dear little Kittie!" she said, lightly. "No one to glance at Susan Erskine would think of fancy-work, for the whole evening. There is nothing in her face or manner, or about her attire, that would suggest the possibility of her knowing anything about fancy matters of any sort. I tell you her face is a strange one. I found myself quoting to my 'inner consciousness' the sentence: 'Life is real, life is earnest,' every time I looked at the lines about her mouth. Whatever else she can or can not do, I am morally certain that she can't crochet. Girls, think of that name — Susan Erskine! Doesn't it sound strangely? How do you suppose it sounds to Ruth? I tell you this whole thing is dreadful! I can't feel reconciled to it. Do you suppose she will have to call that woman mother?"

"What does she call her now?"

"Well, principally she doesn't call her at all. She says 'you' at rare intervals when she has to speak to her, and she said 'she,' when she spoke of her to me; not speaking disagreeably you know, but hesitatingly, as if she did not know what to say, or what would be expected of her. Oh, Ruth does well; infinitely better than I should, in her circumstances, I feel sure. I said as much to that disagreeable Judge Burnham who keeps staying there, for no earthly reason, what I can see, except to complicate Ruth's trials 'How does your friend bear up under it?' he asked me, with an insinuating air, as though he expected me to reveal volumes. 'She bears it royally, just as she always does everything,' I said, and I was dreadfully tempted to add: 'Don't you see how patiently she endures your presence here?' Just as though I would tell him anything about it, if she tore around like a lunatic!"

"Oh, well, now," said Eurie, oracularly, "there are worse crosses in life, I dare say, than Ruth's having to call that woman mother."

"Of course there are; nobody doubts it; the difficulty is that particular type of cross has just now come to her, and while she doesn't have to bear those others which are worse, she *does* have to bear that; and it is a cross, and she needs grace to help her — just exactly as much grace as though there wasn't anyone on earth called on to bear a harder trial. I never could understand why my burnt finger should pain me any the less because somebody else had burned her entire arm."

At this point Flossy interrupted the conversation with one of those innocent, earnest questions which she was always in these days asking, to the no small confusion of some classes of people.

"Are these two women Christians?"

"That I don't know," Marion answered, after staring at the questioner a moment in a half dazed way. "I wondered it, too, I remember. Flossy Shipley, I thought of you while I sat there, and I said to myself, 'She would be certain to make the discovery in less time than I have spent talking with them.' But I don't know how you do those things. What way was there for me to tell? I couldn't sit down beside them and say, 'Are you a Christian?' could I? How is it to be done?"

Flossy looked bewildered.

"Why," she said, hesitatingly, "I don't know. I never thought there was anything strange about it. Why shouldn't those things be talked of as well as any others? You discovered whether the young lady was fond of music and painting. I can't see why it wouldn't have been just as easy to have found out about her interests in more important matters."

"But how would you have done it? Just

suppose yourself to have been in Judge Erskine's parlor, surrounded by all those people who were there last evening, how would you have introduced the subject which is of the most importance?"

"Why," said Flossy, looking puzzled, "how do I know? How can I tell unless I had been there and talked it over? You might as well ask me how I should have introduced the question whether — well, for instance, whether they knew Mr. Roberts, supposing they had come from the same city, and I had reason to think it possible — perhaps probable — that they were his friends. It seems to me I should have referred to it very naturally, and that I should have been apt to do it early in our conversation. Now, you know it is quite possible — if not probable — that they are intimate friends of the Lord Jesus. Why couldn't I have asked them about him?"

Marion and Eurie looked at each other in a sort of puzzled amusement, then Marion said:

"Still I am not sure that you have answered my question about how to begin on such a subject. You know you could have said, 'Did you meet Mr. Roberts in Boston?' supposing them to have been in Boston. But you could hardly say, 'Did you meet the Lord Jesus there?' I am not sure but that sounds irreverent to you. I don't mean it to be; I really want to understand how those subjects present themselves to your mind."

"I don't believe I can tell you," Flossy said, simply. "They have no special way of presenting themselves. It is all so new to me that I suppose I haven't gotten used to it yet. I am always thinking about it, and wondering whether any new people can tell me anything new. Now I am interested in what you told me about that Susan, and I feel as though I should like to ask her whether there were any very earnest Christians where she used to live and whether they had any new ways of reading the Bible, and whether the young ladies had a prayer-meeting, and all those things, you know."

Again Marion and Eurie exchanged glances. This didn't sound abrupt, or out of place, or in any sense offensive to ideas of propriety. Yet who talked in that way among their acquaintances? And *how had* Flossy gotten ahead of them in all these things? It was a standing subject of wonderment among those girls how Flossy had outstripped them.

They were silent for a few minutes. Then Eurie suddenly changed the current of thought: "How strange that these changes should have come to Ruth and we know nothing about it until a mother and sister were actually domiciled! We are all so intimate, too. It seems that there are matters about which we have not learned to talk together."

"Ruth was always more reserved than the rest of us," Flossy said. "I am not so surprised at not knowing about *her* affairs; we are more communicative, I think. At least I have told you all about the changes that are to come to me, and I think you would tell me if you had anything startling, wouldn't you?"

Marion rose up and went over to Flossy, and, bending, kissed her fair cheek.

"You little pink blossom," she said, with feeling, "I'll tell you all the nice things I can think of, one of these days. In the meantime I must go home; and remember, Eurie, you are not to do anything dreadful of any sort without telling Flossy and me beforehand."

"I won't," said Eurie, with a conscious laugh, and the trio separated.

Two hours later Marion Wilbur was the recipient of the following note:

"DEAR MARION:—

"I promised to tell you — though I don't intimate that this comes under your prescribed limit of things 'awful.' Still, I want to tell you. I am almost sorry that I have not been like little Flossy, and talked it all over freely with you. Someway I couldn't seem to. The truth is, I am to be married, in six week's time, to Mr. Harrison. Think of my being a minister's wife! But he is going away from here and perhaps I can learn. There! the ice is broken; now I can tell you about it. Come as soon as you can, and, as Flossy says, 'Have a quiet little confidence.' Lovingly,

"EURIE."

It was about this very hour that Eurie opened

and looked at, in a maze of astonishment and bewilderment, a dainty envelope, of special size and design, from which there fell Marion Wilbur's wedding-cards!

CHAPTER III.

A CROSS OF LEAD.

I DO not know that I need even try to tell you about the succession of petty trials and embarrassments that haunted Ruth Erskine's way during the next few days. They belonged to that class of trials hard to endure — so hard, indeed, that at times the spirit shrinks away in mortal terror, and feels that it can bear no more; and yet in the telling to a listener they dwindle in importance. As for Ruth, she did not *tell* them — she lived them.

Everything was so new; nothing in or about the house could go on according to the old fashion; and yet there was no new fashion shaped.

She saw many a thing which she must not do, and but few things that seemed to bear doing. She must stop in the act of ordering dinner, and remember in confusion that it was not her business to order dinners in this house any more. And yet she must remember that the nominal mistress seemed to know no more about ordering dinners for a family of eight than she knew about ten thousand other things that were waiting for her attention. Poor Ruth struggled and groaned and wondered, and rarely cried, but grew paler, if possible, than before, and her forehead was continually drawn, either with lines of pain or of intense self-suppression. She congratulated herself that her father escaped some of the misery. He went early to his office, shutting the door on the incongruous elements in his household with a sense of relief, and going out into the business world, where everything and everybody were as usual, and returning late, giving as little time to the home puzzle as possible. Yet it wore on him. Ruth could see that, and it but increased her burden to feel that the struggle she made to help was so manifest a *struggle*, and was, in some sense, a failure.

He detained her one morning in the library, with that special word of detention which as yet he had never applied to any one but her.

"My daughter, let me see you a moment before I go out. Do you think we ought to try to have some friends come in, in a social way?"

At this question Ruth stood aghast. Her father's friends had hitherto not been hard for her to entertain — lawyers, judges, professional men of different degrees of prominence, often without their wives, and when the ladies were included they were of an age, as a rule, to expect little in the way of entertainment from Ruth, except a gracious attention to their comfort; so that, beyond very careful directions issued to very competent servants, and a general outlook on the perfected arrangements, little had been expected of her. But now it was different other than professional people would expect invitations; and besides, the hostess was no hostess at all — would not know what to do — and, what was infinitely more painful, what *not* to do.

No wonder that Ruth was appalled over this new duty looming before her. Yet of course it was a *duty;* she flushed over the thought that her father had been obliged to suggest it Of course people were expecting introductions; of course they would call — hosts of them. How much better it would be to have a gathering of a few friends before the great world pounced in upon them, so they might feel that at least with a few the ordeal of introduction was over.

"I don't mean a large party," her father hastened to explain. "Just a few friends — not professional ones, you know, but some of your new acquaintances in the church, perhaps. I thought you might like to have a gathering somewhat like that which you told me of at our little friend, Flossy Shipley's."

If he had not been looking down at the grate, just then, instead of into his daughter's face, he would have seen her start, and almost catch her breath over this suggestion. It was not that she was jealous of little Flossy, for whom her father had shown very special and tender regard ever since the prayer-meeting which he attended in her company, but it came to her with a sudden sense of the change that had fallen upon them. To think that they — the *Erskines* — should be making an attempt to have a social gathering like unto one that Flossy Shipley had planned!

"We couldn't do the things that she did," Ruth said, quickly. "The elements which we would have to bring together would be too incongruous."

"No," he answered, "not exactly like hers, of course, but something simple and informal. I thought your three friends would come, and Dr. Dennis, you know, and people of that stamp, who understand and will help us. Wouldn't it be well to try to do something of the kind, daughter, or doesn't the idea meet with your approval?"

"Oh, yes," she said, drawing in her breath. "Yes, father, we must do something. I will try. But I hardly know how to commence. You know I am not mistress of the house now; it makes it difficult for me."

"I know," he said, and the expression of his face led his daughter instantly to regret that she had made such a remark. It was the life she lived at this time — saying words, and regretting that she had done so. They went on, however, perfecting the arrangements for the social gathering. There had occurred to Ruth an instant

trouble in the way, which was that ever-present
one in the American woman's life — *clothes.*

"We can not hasten this thing," she said.
"There will need to be some shopping done, and
some dress-making — that is, I should think there
would need to be."

She corrected herself, and the embarrassment
involved in the fact that she was not the mistress
of the new comers presented itself. Suppose
they chose to think they had clothes enough, and
proposed to appear in any of the ill-made, badly-
selected materials which seemed to compose their
wardrobe! If they were only two children, that
she might shut up, in a back room up-stairs,
and turn the key on outsiders until such time as
they could be made presentable, what a relief it
would be!

Evidently her father appreciated that embarrassment.

"I tried to arrange that matter before I came
home," he said. "I furnished money, and suggested as well as I could; but it didn't work. I
hardly know what was the trouble. They didn't
understand, or something. Ruth, what can you
do about it? Is there any way of managing?"

Ruth tried to consider, while her cheeks flushed, and her heart beat hard, in what way she could suggest to her father to manage his wife and daughter.

"*Susan* would listen to suggestions, I think," she said, slowly. "But I don't know whether"—

And then she broke off, and recurred to another of the endless trials of this time. If she and her father were to be compelled to hold conversations concerning this woman, it was absolutely necessary that they come to an understanding as to what to call her.

"Father," she said, plunging desperately into the depths of the question. "What am I to call her? Does she—or, do *you*—desire that I should say mother?"

"No," he said, quickly. "Surely not, unless"—

"Well, then," Ruth said, after waiting in vain for him to conclude. "Am I to say 'Mrs. Erskine?'"

"Oh, I don't know."

He spoke in visible agitation, and commenced a nerve-distracting walk up and down the room.

"I don't know anything about any of this mis-

...rable business. Sometimes I am very sorely tempted to wish that I had left everything as it was, and gone on in my old life, and endured the results."

"Don't," said Ruth, aghast at this evidence of desperate feeling, and roused, for a moment, from minor considerations into a higher plane. "Don't feel in this way, father; we will do the best we can, and it will all come out right; at least, we will try to do what is right."

He came over to her then, standing before her, looking into her eyes, and there was that half-appealing look in his which had touched her before.

"Ruth, if we could — if there was any way that we could — manage to *like* them a little, it would make the whole thing so much better, both for them and us."

What an amazing thing to say! what an almost ludicrous thing, when one reflected that he was talking about his *wife!* Yet none knew better than did Ruth that *names* implying love did not make love! How pitiful this appealing sentence was! How could her father ever hope to learn to like this woman, who was his wife? For herself, she had not even thought of such a thing as trying. The most she had planned for was to endure, to tolerate — certainly not to like, most certainly never to *love!* She stood dumbly before her father, having no word of help for him. And presently he turned from her with a sigh; and, when he spoke again, it was in a business-like tone:

"Well, daughter, do the best you can. Manage everything exactly as you have been in the habit of doing. About the dress question, talk with Susan, if you can; tell her what will be proper — what you want done. I will see that her mother follows her directions. For the rest, we will manage some way; we shall have to depend on the kindness of our friends. Judge Burnham will help us in any way he can. He understands matters."

This suggested to Ruth to inquire in regard to him.

"What is Judge Burnham staying in town for? Where is he staying, anyway?"

"Why, he lives in town. He is practicing here. Didn't you know it? He has been absent a long time on professional business. I hardly know how it has happened that you have never met him until now. He has a country-seat ten miles or so away from the city. He is there a good deal, I presume; but he boards now at the Leighton House. He was about changing boarding places when we came home. It was for that reason, among others, that I invited him to stop with us for a few days. You like him, don't you, Ruth?"

This last with a sudden change of tone, and almost anxiety expressed in his manner.

"Oh, yes," said Ruth, half in impatience, as one to whom the subject was too unimportant to stop over. And she was conscious of a flitting determination that, whatever other person she might be called upon to like, she would never trouble herself to make any effort of that sort for *him*.

And then she went away to plan for a party in which she was to be the real head, while appearing before the world only as the dutiful daughter; to plan, also, for the new mother and sister's toilets — whether they would, or not, trusting to her father's authority to make them submissive to her schemes.

A little more talk about that matter of liking people, Ruth was destined to hear; and it developed ideas that bewildered her. It chanced that Flossy Shipley came in for a little chat with Ruth, over the recent astounding news connected with their mutual friend, Marion. It chanced, also, that the new-comers were both up stairs for the evening, Mrs. Erskine being one of those persons who indulge in frequent sick-headaches, during which time her daughter Susan was her devoted slave. So Judge Erskine sat with his daughter, book in hand, because conversation between them was now of necessity on such trying subjects that they mutually avoided it; but he rarely turned a leaf; and he greeted Flossy Shipley with a smile of pleasure, and asked, almost pleadingly, if he might stay and listen to their gossip. Very glad assent, Flossy gave, and emphasized it by talking to Ruth with as much apparent freedom as though he were absent.

"I like it," she said, speaking of Marion. "I think she will make such a perfectly splendid minister's wife."

Flossy still dealt largely in superlatives, and paid very little attention to the grammatical no sition of her adjectives. "I am almost sorry that I am not going to live here, so I could have the benefit of her; she will be just as full of helpful plans for people! And when she gets in a position to influence them you will see how much good she can do. Ruth, were you very much surprised?"

"Greatly so. I imagined that she did not even admire Dr. Dennis very much. I don't know that she ever gave me reason to think so, except by being silent sometimes, when I expected her to speak; but of course that is accounted for now. Isn't the marriage sudden?"

"More sudden than they had planned," Flossy said. "Dr. Dennis found it necessary to be absent just then on a matter of business, and to go West, just in the direction they had proposed to go together, and he was obliged to be absent for some time, which would give him little chance for vacation later in the season, and, in short," said Flossy, with a bright smile, "I think if they would own it, they were very lonely, and very anxious to enjoy each other's society, and thought they were wasting time, and set about finding reasons why they should change their plans. You know reasons can almost always be found for things, when we are very anxious to find them!"

"Is that so!" Judge Erskine asked, looking up from his book, and speaking in so earnest a tone that both girls turned toward him inquiringly. "Do you mean to say that if one were anxious to change — well, say his opinion of a person, he could bring himself to do it on reasonable grounds?"

It was a curious question, and to Ruth it was a very embarrassing one. Her cheeks flushed painfully, and her eyes drooped to the bit of fancy work which lay idly in her lap.

"That wasn't quite what I was thinking about," Flossy said, gently and seriously, as one who realized that his question reached deeper than he meant her to understand. "But I do truly think, sir, that if we feel as though we *ought* to change our opinion of a person, we can set seriously about doing it and accomplish it."

"In that case, you would not believe it necessary to have any enemies in this world, would you?"

"Not real enemies, I think, though I wouldn't

want to be friends, of course, with everybody. But — well, Judge Erskine, I can't explain to you what I mean. I don't know how to reason, you see. All I can do is to tell you what really occurred. There is a person whom I disliked; he was very trying to me, and I had to be thrown in his society very often, and I knew I ought to feel differently toward him, because, you know, I couldn't hope to be of the least help to him, unless I felt differently. So I set myself earnnestly to trying, and I succeeded. I have the kindest possible feelings toward him, and I think I am gaining a little influence."

During this recital Flossy's fair, peach-blossom cheek had taken a deeper shade, and her eyes drooped low. She was giving what Judge Erskine felt was a bit of heart-history, and he did not know that she realized any personal application. How should the innocent little mouse know anything about his affairs?

"Do you mind telling me how you set to work to accomplish this change?" he asked, and his daughter knew that his voice was almost husky.

"First," said Flossy, simply and gravely, "I prayed for him; I gave all my soul to a desire for his conversion; I prayed to be shown how to help him — how to act toward him; then I prayed for grace to like him, to be interested in him, and to overlook his faults, or his failings; and then — why, I am not sure there is any 'then' to it. It is all told in that word 'prayer.' The Lord Jesus helped me, Judge Erskine; that is the whole of it."

"Do you really think we have a right to pray about the matter of our likes and dislikes?" There was no mistaking the earnestness in Judge Erskine's voice this time.

Flossy turned wondering eyes on him, as she said, "Oh, yes, indeed! The direction is, 'Casting all your care upon him,' and that is a real care, you know." Ah! *didn't* Judge Erskine know? "And then He says, 'In *everything* by prayer and supplication, let your requests be made known.' I couldn't doubt my right. Indeed it seemed to me to be a duty, not only to pray, but actually to supplicate, to coax, you know, just as I was so tempted to do when a child. It seemed blessed to me to think that the Lord Jesus took such minute notice of our human nature that he knew it would help us to be al lowed to keep a subject constantly before him, and to keep coaxing about it. Don't you think that is wonderful, Judge Erskine?"

"Wonderful!" repeated Judge Erskine, in a moved tone, and he arose and began that pacing up and down the room, which always with him indicated deep feeling. Ruth and Flossy presently continued their talk in a lower tone, until Judge Erskine came toward them again and said, "I will bid you good-night, I think, and thank you, my dear young lady. Your words are strong and helpful; don't forget them in any future experience of life that you may have; perhaps they will help you through deep waters, some day."

Then he went to the library. As for Ruth, she sought her room with two thoughts following her: one, that Flossy had been to her father what *she* had failed in being — a helper; and the other, that possibly she might pray herself into a different state of feeling toward this woman and this girl, who were to her now only heavy, *heavy* crosses.

CHAPTER IV.

BITTER HERBS.

THE morning of the night which had closed in gloom, opened to Ruth Erskine with a faint promise of better things. Not so much that, either; rather, she resolved on heroism. The sun shone, and the air was fresh with the breath of coming spring. The outlook seemed more hopeful. Ruth resolved upon trying Flossy's way. She would pray about this matter; she would nerve herself for duty and trial: she would bear whatever of disagreeableness came athwart her plans. No matter how obstinate or offensive this new woman proved herself to be on the question of wardrobe, she would bravely face the ordeal, and do what she could. No amount of offensiveness should cause her to lose self-control. It was childish and useless to yield in this way, and let inevitable trials crush one. She did not mean to do it. Her father should see that she could be as strong over *real* trials, as Flossy Shipley could be over imaginary ones; for what had that little kitten ever had to try her? This Ruth said, with a curl of her handsome upper lip.

She went about her morning duties with something like the briskness of her old life, and settled herself to Bible-reading, resolved on finding something to help her. She had not yet learned the best ways of reading in the Bible; indeed, she had not given that subject the attention which Flossy had. To begin a chapter, and read directly and seriously through it, getting what information she could, was the most that she, as yet, knew about the matter. And the chapter occurring next to the one that she read yesterday was the fifth of Romans: "Therefore being justified by faith, we have peace with God through our Lord Jesus Christ: by whom also we have access by faith into this grace wherein we stand, and rejoice in hope of the glory of God. And not only so, but we glory in tribulations also; knowing that tribulation worketh patience; and patience, experience; and experience, hope." Thus on, through the solemn and wonderful chapter, heeding the words indeed; getting some sort of idea of St. Paul's meaning, and yet not making his experience personal, in the least; not realizing that the sentence, "We have peace with God," included Ruth Erskine; not seeing, at least, that it was a present promise, referring to present experience; not realizing anything, save a desire to be armed for unpleasant and continuous duties, and a dim idea that reading the Bible was one of the preparations which were given her to make. In much the same spirit, she knelt to pray. She was humble, she was reverent, she was in earnest, she prayed for strength, for wisdom, for patience; and the words were strictly proper, and in accordance with the desires. The prayer, to a listener, would have breathed the spirit of confidence and faith; yet it must be confessed that Ruth Erskine arose from her knees without any sense of having really communed with

Christ, without any realization of his presence, and without any very definite expectation of receiving actual, practical benefit from the exercise. She did not realize the feeling, and yet she possessed somewhat of the same spirit of the child who prayed: "Dear Jesus, help me to be good to-day. I know I can be good if I try, and I intend to try; but you can help me if you want to!" Remember, I do not say that she realized it; but that does not alter the fact that she went out from her room, to meet the trials of the day, strong in the strength of her own resolves. She repaired at once to Mrs. Judge Erskine's room, determined to be very composed and patient, and to combat whatever disagreeable or dissenting thing might be said with forbearance and kindness.

Mrs. Erskine's objection to new and fine clothing must be overcome, but it should be done wisely. She resolved to say nothing to Susan beforehand. She would not admit, even to herself, that her father's evident confidence in Susan's powers was a trial to her; but, all the same, she determined to show him that she, too, had powers, and that she could manage matters without Susan's help.

Alas for Ruth! Mrs. Erskine was not in the least averse to fine feathers. She was not lofty, nor angry, nor hurt; she was good-naturedly and ungrammatically and exasperatingly loquacious. It would have been much easier for Ruth to endure ill-temper. She was nerved for that. Unconsciously she had planned for and prayed for self-control, to enable her to endure, not what she would meet in Mrs. Erskine, but what she would have had to contend with in herself, had she been in Mrs. Erskine's place; and as, given the same circumstances, the two would act in a totally different manner, failure was inevitable.

"Come in," said Mrs. Erskine, heartily, in answer to Ruth's low knock. "Land alive! come right in, don't stop to rap. What's the use of being so particular with one's folks? I been a wishin' you would run in and have a chat. I was tellin' your pa, only last night, how chirk and nice we could all be here, if you would be sort of sociable, you know, and not so stiff and proud-like. Not that you mean to be proud, I s'pose; Susan says you don't. She says it's natural for some folks to be haughty. I s'pose it is. But, land alive! I'm glad I'm not one of them kind. Haughty folks always did shrivel me right up. Set down here by the fire. I think these grates is real comfortable. I told your pa, last night, that I wouldn't have shivered over an old barn of a wood-stove, all these years, if I'd known what comfortable things there was in the world. How dreadful pale you look! Is it natural for you to look so like a ghost all the time?"

"I am not accustomed to having a great deal of color in my face, I believe," Ruth answered, sitting squarely and stiffly in the most uncomfortable chair she could find in the room, and feeling, just then, that to be an actual ghost would be a positive relief.

"Well, now, I don't believe it's nature for any human being to be so like a sheet as that. If I was your pa, I'd have you through a course of medicine in less than no time. You need strengthenin' up. You ought to have some Peruvian bark, or some quassia chips, or some kind of bitter stuff steeped up for you to drink

It would do you a power of good, I know it would. You jest let me fix you up a mess, like I do Susan, and see what it'll do for you. S'prise your pa with the change in you, I dare say."

Poor Ruth! She felt as though stuff that was bitter enough had been mixed and steeped, and held to her lips, and that she was being obliged to drink it to the very dregs. *Did* she need it? Was it possible that the Divine Physician saw her need of such bitter herbs as these which had fallen to her lot? She started, and even flushed a little over the sudden thought. *She* did not believe it. This was her *father's* sin, not hers. It had only fallen upon her because of the old, solemn law: "'The iniquities of the fathers shall be visited upon the children." She hurried her thoughts away from it It would not do to sit in that room, with that woman staring at her, and indulge in questionings like these.

"I came in to see if I could be of any assistance to you in the way of shopping. You will need something new, I suppose, before the gad

ering of friends which my father proposes to have."

Ruth had decided to take it as a matter of course that new garments were to be bought, and thus forestall, if she could, haughty objections. She need not have been thus careful. Mrs. Erskine had stated truly that she was not one of the "haughty" sort. She had no objection to any number of new dresses, and to their being made as elaborately as possible.

"Now you speak of it, I dare say I do," she said, leaning back complacently in her comfortable little rocker. "In fact, your pa spoke of that very thing this morning. He said like enough you would 'tend to it, and he filled my pocket-book up handsome. There ain't a stingy streak about your pa. I knew that, years and years ago, when he was a young man. It was the very first thing that drawed me to him — the free kind of way in which he threw around his money. It seemed so noble-like, specially when I was drivin' every nerve to keep soul and body together, and lived among folks that didn't dare to say their bodies was their own, for fear they would have 'em seized on for debt, and took to jail. I tell you that was livin'! You don't know nothing about it, and I hope to the land that you never will."

What could Ruth do but groan inwardly, and wish that her father had been, in his youth, the veriest miser that ever walked the earth! Anything, so that this terrible woman would not have been "drawed" to him. She tried to hurry the question:

"What have you thought of getting?" she asked, nervously twisting and untwisting the tassels of the tidy against which she leaned, and feeling disagreeably conscious that a glow of color had mounted to her very temples in her efforts at self-control.

"Land alive, I don't know. I've thought of a dozen different dresses since your pa told me this morning what he wanted. He wants things to be awful nice, I can see that; and why shouldn't he? A man that's got money and is free with it has a right to say what he will have, I'm sure. I think it ought to be something bright, like something — well, *bridie*, you know."

This last with such a distressing little simper that it was almost more than Ruth could do to keep from rushing from that awful room, and declaring to her father that she would have no more to do with this thing. He should fight his dreadful battles alone. But outwardly she held still, and the shrill, uncultured little voice went on:

"You see I *am* almost like a bride, meeting your pa's friends so for the first time, though land knows it is long enough ago that I planned what to wear when I should meet 'em. It took longer to get ready than I expected."

There was not even a spice of bitterness in this sentence. If there had been — if there had been a suggestion that this woman felt somewhat of her own wrongs, Ruth thought that she could have borne it better. But the tone was simply contemplative, as of one who was astonished, in a mild way, over the tragedy that life had managed to get up for her.

"You see," she continued, "I hadn't a chance for much dressin' or thinkin' about it; your pa was so weak that I had about all I could do to fix bitters and things, and manage to keep the breath of life in his body. And many's the time when I thought he'd beat, and die right before my face and eyes in spite of me. Then he went off on that journey afore he was able, and I've always believed, and always shall, that he didn't rightly know what he was about after that, for quite a spell. So now I think more than likely it would please him to have things kind of gay and lively. I ain't said anything about it to Susan — she ha'n't no special interest in dressing up, anyway, and she and I don't always agree about what looks nice, but I think your pa would like it if I had a green silk — bright, rich green, you know, nothing dull and fady. I saw one when I was a girl — fact is, I sewed on it — and it was for a bride, too, and I said to myself then, says I, ' If *I'm* ever a bride, I'll have a dress as much like this as two peas.' I've been a good while about it, but that's neither here nor there. I've got a beautiful red bow; that wide, rich-looking kind of ribbon; a woman give it to me for tending up to her poor girl afore she died. She had the consumption, and I took care of her off and on a good share of the fall, and she give me this ribbon. It's real nice, though land knows I didn't want pay for doing things for her poor girl. 'Twan't *pay*, neither, for the matter of that; it was just to show they felt grateful, you know, and I've always set store by that ribbon. I've never wore it, because Susan she thought it wan't suited to our way of livin" and no more it wan't, though we lived nice enough in a small way. Your pa never skimped us on money, though, land alive! I didn't dream of his havin' things about him like he has, and I was always for tryin' to lay up, 'cause I didn't know how much money he had, and I didn't know but he'd come to poverty some day. Rich folks do, and I was for savin', and Susan didn't object. Susan is a good girl as ever was. And so the red bow is just as nice as ever it was — not a mite soiled nor nothing, and I think it would go lovely with a green silk dress, don't you?"

"No," said Ruth, severely and solemnly. Not another word could she have forced her white lips to say, and I don't know how to explain to you what awful torture this talk was to her. The truth is, to those of you who do not, because of a fine subtle, inner sympathy, understand it already, it is utterly unexplainable

"Land alive!" said Mrs. Erskine, startled by the brief, explosive answer, and by the white, set lips, "don't you? Now, I thought you would. You dress so like a picture yourself, I thought you would know all about it, and your pa said you knew what was what as well as the next one."

Think of Judge Erskine's aristocratic lips delivering such a sentence as that!

"Now, I had a geranium once, when I was a girl. It was the only pretty thing I had in the world, and I set store by it, for more reasons than one. It was give to me by my own aunt on my father's side. It was pretty nigh all she had to give, poor thing! They was dreadful poor like the rest of us, and she give me this the very winter she died. I had it up in my room, and it kept a blowing and blowing all winter long — I never see the like of that thing to blow! And I used to stand and look at it, just between daylight and dark. It stood right by my one window, where the last streak of daylight come in, and I used to squeeze in there between the table and the wall to make my button-holes, and when it got so dark I jest couldn't take another stitch, I'd stand and look at the thing all in blow, and I thought I never see anything so pretty in all my life, and I made up my mind then and there, that a green silk dress, about the color of them leaves, and a red ribbon about the color of them blossoms, would be the prettiest thing to wear in the world. I got the bow a good many years ago, and I was always kind of savin' on it up, waiting for the dress." Just here there was the faintest little breath of a sigh. "But, then, if you don't think it would be the thing, why I'm willing to leave it to you. Your pa said you'd see that everything was ship-shape."

"I think," said Ruth, and her voice was hollow, even to herself, "I think that my father's taste would be a plain, black silk, with white lace at the throat. If you desire to please him, I am sure you will make that choice."

"Why!" exclaimed Mrs. Judge Erskine, and she couldn't help looking a bit dismayed. "Land alive! do you think so? Black! why it will make folks think of a funeral, won't it?"

"No," said Ruth, "black is worn on all occasions by persons who know enough to wear it."

Then she arose. She had reached the utmost limit of endurance. Another sentence from this woman she felt would have driven her wild. Yet she was doomed to hear one more before she closed the door after herself.

"Well, now, if you honestly think it will be best, I s'pose I'll agree to it, as your pa seemed to think things must go your way. But I don't quite like it, jest because it seems kind of bad luck. I don't believe them notions about black clothes at merry-makings, you know, though when I was a girl folks honestly thought so, and it seems kind of pokerish to run right into 'em. I never would begin to clean house of a Friday — some bad luck was sure to come; and as for seein' the moon over my left shoulder, I won't do it, *now* — not if I can help it. But black silk ain't so funeral as bombazine and such, and I s'pose —"

Here Ruth slammed the door, and put both trembling hands to her ears, and ran across the hall to the refuge of her own room, and closed, and locked, and *bolted* her door.

As for Mrs. Erskine, she relapsed of necessity into silence, and for the space of five minutes ceased her rocking and looked meditatively into the glowing grate. Then she arose, and for the second time that morning her speech was heralded by the breath of a sigh, as she said aloud. "I ain't no ways certain that I can ever make head or tail to that girl." Then she went to her new and elegant dressing-bureau, and opened a drawer, and drew from under a pile of snowy clothing a little box, and took therefrom, wrapped in several folds of tissue paper, the treasured bow. She had kept it choicely for fourteen years, always with a dim sense of feeling that the time might come when life would so have opened to her that she would be able to add to it the green silk dress, and appear in triumph. Besides, it represented to her so much gratitude and affection, and there was actually on her small, worn, withered face, the suspicion of a tear, as she carefully folded and replaced it. Her audible comment was: "A black silk dress and a white lace bow! land alive!"

CHAPTER V.

SEEKING HELP.

FOR the rest of the day Ruth was in gloom; indeed, I might almost say she was in despair. In a dim, dreary sort of way, she felt that her refuge had failed her. If it really was not going to help her to read in the Bible and pray, what *was* she to do? Now, I do not mean that she suddenly lost faith in the Bible, or in prayer, but simply that despairing thoughts, like these, ran riot through her brain, and she gave them attention; also, she felt as though any effort to help, or any attempt to like these people — nay, even to tolerate them — was impossible. Mrs. Erskine's good-natured coarseness of tone and speech, her horrible arrangement of words and phrases, her frequent allusions to "your pa," in the free, careless tone which indicated a partnership of interest between them, were all so many horrors to the refined, reserved, low-voiced daughter.

"I will just shut myself into my room," she said, pacing back and forth like a caged lion. "I will not try to associate with them; it can never be done; they can not be improved; there is no hope in that direction: there is nothing to build on. I must just take care of myself, and see to it that I do not sink to their level."

Carrying out this plan, or, rather, allowing herself to glide along with it, she turned away with almost a shiver from her father's question, that evening, addressed to her in a low tone, as the family were leaving the dining-room:

"Daughter, shall we try to go to prayer-meeting to-night?"

The first prayer-meeting since this invasion into their home! Ruth had not forgotten it; instead, she had been looking forward all day to that meeting, as a refuge for her storm-tossed soul. Without giving really definite thought to it, she yet felt that there, at least, would be help and comfort; and not once had it occurred to her that the new-comers must be invited to attend. She realized, now, with a throb of pain, that it was this sense of fleeing from their presence which had helped to give pleasantness to the thought of the meeting. Was it possible that "*they*" must be taken?

"Father, I can't," she said, turning and facing him with glowing face and defiant eyes. "I have tried to-day to help, and have been an awful failure. I just feel as though I could not endure it. No, I say, let us stay at home with our misery, and not parade it before a gaping world. No, I am not going to prayer-meeting to-night."

Her father turned from her, and walked, without another word, to the library, whither, according to the new rules of the house, they went directly after tea, for prayer. Ruth could not help noticing that her father's tall, handsome form stooped, as though he were bowed with suddenly-added years. The moment those words were spoken, she felt that she would have given worlds to have unsaid them; but to take back what has been said in haste and folly is oftentimes an impossible task. She chose the darkest corner of the library, and felt that, if she could have crouched in it, out of sight forever, it would have been happiness. Her father's voice, as he read the psalm for the evening, was low and tremulous. He had by no means gotten used to these new duties — had not felt their comfort, nor recognized in them a help. As yet he was in the realm of hard *duty*. His prayer touched Ruth as no prayer had ever done before. It opened the fountains of tears. On rising from her knees, she turned quickly to the window, to hide her disturbed face, and to determine whether she should follow her father from the room, and apologizing for the hard, unhelpful words which she had spoken, say that, of course, they must go to prayer-meeting. He did not wait for her tardy resolution, but turned at once to his wife :

"Will you and Susan accompany me to our weekly meeting? I feel that we need all the help we can get, and that is one of the sources of supply."

Susan answered promptly, and with a glad

ring in her voice that he could not have failed to notice. She was so glad to hear that this was the evening for the meeting. She had been thinking about it to-day, and wondering whether it were, and whether she could go. As for the mother, she said, hesitatingly:

"Why, yes," she supposed so. There was nothing to hinder, that she knew of. She was no great hand for going out evenings, though, to be sure, going out in a city, where the walks were good and the streets as light as day, was a different affair from blundering along in the dark, as *she* had been obliged to do. Susan always went to prayer-meeting; but she hadn't never went in her life, as she knew of; but then, of course, if *he* wanted to go, she would go along.

It was not possible, apparently, for Mrs. Erskine to answer a question briefly. She was full of reminiscences. They went to prayer-meeting — "father and mother and daughter." Ruth said this sentence over after they were all gone — said it as she listened to the sound of their retreating footsteps — her father, and all the mother she had ever known, and their daughter

She was left out! Her father had not given her opportunity to change her mind. He had simply said, as they passed out, "I am sorry, daughter, that you do not feel like accompanying us." If he had but said, "Daughter, won't you go?" she would have choked down the tears and answered, "Yes." But she could not bring her pride, or her grief, to make this concession. She honestly did not know whether to call it pride or grief.

Bitterly sorry was she to miss the prayer-meeting. She began to feel that, even with those two present, it might have helped her. So sorry was she that, had she dared to traverse the streets alone, she would have made ready and followed. While she still stood, looking out drearily, too sad now even for tears, the bell sounded through the quiet house, and, giving little heed to it, she was presently startled by the advent of Judge Burnham.

"Thomas thought no one was in," he said, coming toward her, after an instant's surprised pause, "and I ventured to avail myself of your father's cordial invitations, and come in to consult a book which he has, and I haven't."

It was well for Judge Burnham's peace of mind that he had not come in expecting to see Ruth. She was in the mood to resent such an intrusion, but since it was only books that he wanted, he was welcome. She motioned toward the rows and rows of solemn-looking volumes, as she said:

"Help yourself, Judge Burnham, and make yourself as comfortable as you can. My father's friends are always welcome to his library."

Then Judge Burnham said a strange and unexpected word. Standing there, looking at her with those keen, grave eyes of his, thinking, apparently, not of books at all, he said:

"I wish I could help *you*."

Something in the tone and something in the emphasis caused a vivid blush to spread over Ruth's face. She commenced a haughty sentence:

"Thank you; I am sure it is kind; but —" She was about to say, "but, I do not feel in need of help."

She was stopped by the swift realization that this was not true. She felt, in one sense, in deeper need of help than she had ever done before. Her voice faltered over the words, and finally she stopped, her eyes drooping as they were not wont to droop before others, and those traitorous tears shone in them again. The tearful mood was as foreign to her usual self as possible, and she felt afraid to trust herself to speak further. Besides, what could she say?

Judge Burnham spoke again, earnestly, respectfully:

"I hope you will forgive my intrusion of sympathy, but I do feel for you — perhaps in a way that you can hardly appreciate. There are circumstances in my own hard life that serve to make me in deep sympathy with your present trial. Besides, your father has confided in me fully, and I knew *your* mother. When I was a boy of fourteen she was a woman, young and beautiful and good. She helped me in a hundred of those nameless ways in which a woman can help a motherless boy. If there was any way in which I could serve her daughter it would give me sincerest pleasure to do so."

He was so frank and sincere and grave that Ruth could hardly help being sincere also.

"I need help," she said, raising her eyes for

an instant to his, "but I do not imagine that you, or any human being, can give it me. I shall have to get a victory over my own heart before anything can help me. I am ashamed of myself, and disheartened. Things that I mean to do I utterly fail in, and things that above all others I don't intend to do I drop into, almost of necessity, it seems to me."

What a pity that this man, who wanted to help, had not been familiar with the old-time cry of the sin-sick soul, " For the good that I would I do not, but the evil which I would not that I do." But he was not familiar with that book of the law of the human heart. Still he essayed to comfort.

"I think you are too hard on yourself. I told you that your father had made a confidant of me, and among other things he has repeatedly told me what a help and strengthener you were to him. He said that he never would have been able to carry this hard matter through but for your strong, unselfish words. It was of you he thought most, and when you were unselfish he felt that he could be."

Ruth needed this crumb of comfort and yet it

had its bitter side, and brought another rush of tears.

"He will never speak such words again," she said, and her voice trembled. "I have failed him utterly. To-night he asked me to go to the prayer-meeting, and I refused. I said I could never go out with them anywhere, and that we ought to stay at home and hide our shame."

And having broken through the wall of reserve to this degree poor Ruth gave way utterly, and dropped into a chair, weeping bitterly. Presently she said:

"I would give the world to be able to take it back again; but I can't. I should have gone to the meeting to-night — there was no excuse. I have dishonored my Saviour as well as my father."

Judge Burnham looked down at her in perplexed dismay. No definite purpose had been in his mind, beyond a very strange sympathy for her, and a desire to show it. But he did not in the least know how to deal with tears, nor with trouble which reached to so deep and solemn a place in the heart as this. He was one of those reverent, correct moralists, professing to honor the Bible as a very wise and a very good book, professing to respect religion and honor the name of God; and knowing no more about any of these subjects than that profession indicates when it goes no farther. How was he to comfort one whose bitterest tears were being shed because she had dishonored the Lord? He waited irresolute for a moment, then, as if a sudden and very brilliant thought had struck him, his face brightened.

"If that prayer-meeting would really be a source of help to you, Miss Erskine," and he tried not to have his tone appear incredulous, though at that very moment he was occupied in wondering what it could possibly do for her, "why not reconsider your decision and attend it? I will see you safely there with pleasure, and I presume your coming would gratify your father in his present mood."

For, to this man, the religion of his old friend Judge Erskine was simply a "mood," which he expected to be exchanged presently for some other fancy.

Ruth looked up quickly. Was there possibly an escape from this torture of self-reproach? Was there a chance to show her father that she was bitterly ashamed of herself?

"Isn't it too late?" she asked, and the eagerness in her voice was apparent.

"Oh, no, I should think not," and Judge Burnham drew his watch. "I am not very well versed in the ways of these gatherings, but if it were a lecture, or concert, it is not enough past the hour to cause remark. I am quite willing to brave criticism in that respect, if you say so."

Had Ruth been less engrossed with the affairs of her own troubled heart she would have taken in the strangeness of this offer on Judge Burnham's part to accompany her to a prayer-meeting. Truth to tell he could have echoed Mrs. Erskine's statement, that "she hadn't never went in her life as she knew of." He smiled now over the newness of his position, and yet he cared very little about it. There *were* matters in which Judge Burnham had moral courage enough to face the whole world. To appear in a social meeting with Judge Erskine's daughter was one of them. As for Ruth, true to her nature, she thought nothing about it, but made ready with a speed and an eagerness that would have amazed her attendant, could he have seen her.

So it came to pass that the First Church prayer-meeting again had a sensation. The prayer-room was quite full. Since the revival there had been none of those distressing meetings composed of a handful of the most staid members of the church, but on this particular evening there were more present than usual. There were some who were not in the habit of being seen there, even of late. Shall I venture to tell the reason? The simple truth is, that Dr. Dennis and Marion Wilbur's wedding-cards were out. As Eurie Mitchell has before told you, many things had conspired to make their change of plans advisable, and so, instead of being married in the front-room of the old western farm-house, according to Marion's fancy, the ceremony was to take place in the First Church on the following evening, and every member of that church, young and old, large and small, had received a special invitation to be present.

Now, it is a mistake to suppose that general gossip is confined to small villages and towns, where everybody knows everybody's business better than he knows it himself. I think the experience of others will testify to the truth of the statement that gossip runs riot everywhere. In the larger towns or cities, it runs in eddies, or circles. This clique, or this set, or this grade of society, is, to a man and woman, as deeply interested in what the particular circle are to *do*, or *wear*, or *be*, next, as though they lived in a place measuring three square miles. So, while there were those in this nameless city of which we write, who said, when they heard of the coming ceremony: "Dr. Dennis! Why he is pastor of the First Church, isn't he? or is it the Central Church? Who is Marion Wilbur? does anybody know?" And while there were those who rushed to and fro through the streets of the city, passing under the shadow of the great First Church, who did not know that there was to be a wedding there, who could not tell you the name of the pastor of the church, nor even whether it had a pastor or not, and who had never heard of Marion Wilbur in their lives, and never would, till those lives were ended, though some of them brushed past her occasionally, there were undeniably those who hurried through their duties this evening, or shook off their weariness, or *ennui*, or deferred other engagements and made it convenient to go to the First Church prayer-meeting, for no better reasons than a curious desire to see whether Dr. Dennis would appear any different from usual on the night before his marriage, and whether Marion would be out, and whether she *could* look as unconscious and unconcerned as she always had, and also what she *would wear!* whether she would cling to that old brown dress to the very last! and whether Grace Dennis would be present, and whether she would sit with Marion as they remembered she had, several times, or where? These, and a dozen other matters of equal importance and interest, had actually contributed to the filling of the seats in the First Church chapel! Well, there are worse absorptions than even these. I am not certain that there was a disagreeable word or thought connected with these queries, and yet how sad a thing to think that the Lord of the vineyard is actually indebted to such trivialities for the ingathering of the workers in his vineyard to consult with him as to the work? Alas! alas!

many of them were not workers at all, but drones.

After all, since a higher motive could not touch these people, shall we not be glad that any motive, so long as it was not actually a *sinful* one, brought them within the sound of prayer and praise? They were there anyway, and the service was commenced, and the hymn that followed the pastor's prayer was being sung, when the opening door revealed to the surprised gazers the forms of Ruth Erskine and Judge Burnham! Now Judge Burnham was one who would, on no account, have exerted himself to see how Dr. Dennis would appear, or how Marion Wilbur would dress, since none of these motives moved him. The question was, What had?

CHAPTER VI.

FROM DIFFERENT STANDPOINTS.

ALTHOUGH the First Church prayer meeting had gone several steps onward, gotten beyond the region of distressing pauses, wherein the embarrassed people looked at each other and wished something would happen, it was by no means the free, social, enjoyable gathering that a prayer-meeting ought to be. A lifelong education of too rigid propriety — in other words, false propriety — is not to be overcome in an hour. Therefore, after those who were more accustomed to occupying the time had filled their space there came a lull, not long, not distressing. Those Chautauqua girls were all pres-

out, and any one of them would have led in a hymn rather than let the pause stretch out. But it was long enough for people to wonder whether the hour was not almost gone, and whether there were any others who would get their lips open that evening; and then they heard a strange voice: clear, steady, well-managed, as one accustomed to the sound of her own voice, even in public places, and it belonged to the stranger sitting beside Judge Erskine — none other than his daughter Susan. The words she uttered were these: "Therefore being justified by faith, we have peace with God, through our Lord Jesus Christ."

Now, if it is your fortune to be a regular attendant at a prayer-meeting where a woman's voice is never heard, you can appreciate the fact that the mere recitation of a Bible verse, by a "sister" in the church, was a startling, almost a bewildering innovation. Only a few months before, I am not sure but some of the good people would have been utterly overwhelmed by such a proceeding. But they had received many shocks of late. The Spirit of God coming into their midst had swept away many of their former ideas, and therefore they bore this better.

But the voice went on, clear, steady, as well sustained as though it belonged to a deacon in the church. "I have been all day," it said, "dwelling under the shadow of that verse, 'Peace with God!' It expresses *so* much! Peace is greater than joy, or comfort, or rest. I think the words come to perplexed lives with such power. When we do not see the way clearly; when we are beset with difficulties; when disappointments thicken around us, we can still look up to God and say, 'Up there, where Father is, it is peace.' He sees the way plainly and He will lead us right through the thickets to the sunlight of His eternal presence. I felt this verse specially one day. Something occurred in which I had to bear a prominent part. For a time I was perplexed — was not sure what was right — and, afterward, my friends thought that I did not make the right decision, and I felt afraid that perhaps I had not, and it troubled me. Then I rested my heart on this word: '*justified.*' Not because I have done right; not because my judgment is correct; not because of any act of mine in any direction save that one of trusting in my Lord, justified by *faith!* I am so glad that however much we may disappoint and try our friends, and our own hearts, in the sight of the great and wise and pure God, we are justified through Jesus Christ."

Simple words were these, simply and quietly spoken. The speaker had spent all her life in one place and all her Christian life in one church. In that church it had been her custom to give her word of testimony. Sometimes it was a verse of a hymn that she recited, sometimes it was a text of Scripture, sometimes it was a touch of her own experience. She had grown up with the custom. She did not realize that there were any who had not. It did not occur to her that to the ears of the First Church people this might be a strange sound. So there had been no flutter or embarrassment, no self-consciousness of any sort; simply out of the fullness of her heart she had spoken. The effect on those about her was obvious and various. Judge Erskine's hand, that rested on the knob of his gold-headed cane, trembled visibly; Mrs. Senator Seymour, who sat behind him, looked indignant, and felt that Judge Erskine had had enough to endure before this, but this was really too much! Marion Wilbur, who was present, and who *did* wear her old brown dress, "sticking to it to the very last," sat erect, with glowing cheeks and eyes that were bright with excitement. To fully understand her excitement I shall have to tell you about a little conversation she had just before starting for church.

"Marion," Dr. Dennis had said, as he waited in the stuffy parlor for her to draw on her gloves, "I wish you were a very brave young woman, and liked innovations, and were willing to make a startling one to-night."

"Which you believe I am not, and will not, I conclude," she had replied, laughing; and stopping before him with a mock bow, added:

"Thank you; I believe you are correct about part of it, at least. I certainly feel very meek and quiet to-night, whatever I may have been in the past. What do you want done?"

"I want to get rid of a horrible stiffness that is creeping over our meeting. We have been thawed, but not sufficiently; that is — well, Marion, the prayer-meeting doesn't and *never did*, meet my ideal. It is not social enough —

friendly and familiar enough. I would like to have it a place where we meet together to talk over religious subjects, in exactly the same way that we talk of other matters of interest. I would like, for instance, to ask you as to your opinion of a passage of Scripture, or a hymn; and I should like you to answer as freely as you would if we were sitting with other friends in — say *your* parlor, for instance."

The emphasis in this latter sentence brought a vivid blush to Marion's face, and a little exclamation, not exactly of dismay:

"I think *you* are in a very startling mood. What would your good pillars in the church say to such innovations, do you suppose? It takes my breath away even to think of such a thing! I would almost as soon arise in the desk, and undertake to preach a sermon."

"Which is a very different thing," Dr. Dennis said, stoutly. "But, now, just look at it, Marion. Isn't that the reasonable way to do? Imagine a party of us meeting to discuss a prospective journey to Europe, or to the Holy Land; and, supposing me to be the leader, imagine all the ladies sitting perfectly mum, and the gentlemen only speaking when I called them by name, as if, instead of a social meeting, where all the people were on the same level, it was a catechetical class, met for examination, with myself for examiner! I don't believe we have the true idea of prayer-meetings."

"Perhaps not. But, if I should suddenly say to you, when we are fairly seated in the chapel, 'Dr. Dennis, what do you think is the meaning of the sentence — Called to be *saints?*' what would you think?"

"I should be delighted — positively delighted; and I should proceed to answer you as well as I could; and should like to say, 'Judge Erskine, isn't that your idea?' or, 'Mrs. Chester, what do you think about it?' and thus from one to another, freely, familiarly as we would if we were gathered to converse about anything else that was worthy of our attention. That is my idea of a social prayer-meeting."

"Well," said Marion, "I don't believe you will ever realize your idea. For myself, I should just as soon think of attempting to fly. The minute you get seated behind that great walnut box, with those solemn-looking cushions towering before you, I feel as far removed from you as though miles of space divided us."

"That is just it," Dr. Dennis said, growing eager. "I tell you, this sense of distance and dignity, and unwise solemnity, are all wrong. The barriers ought to be broken down. How I wish, Marion, that you felt it in your heart to help me. I wish you would open your mouth in that meeting to-night. It would do you and me, and everybody good. We should have made a beginning toward getting nearer to the people. I don't mean anything formidable, you know. Suppose you should just recite a verse of Scripture — something appropriate to the subject before us? I don't believe you have an idea of the effect it would have."

"Oh, yes I have," Marion said, with an emphatic nod of her head. "*I* can realize that the effect would be tremendous. I don't believe *you* have the slightest idea of it! What effect will it have, if you and I reach the meeting ten minutes past the time?"

Whereupon they went to church. Of course Marion was interested in Susan Erskine's verse, and Susan Erskine's comments; not so interested that she felt moved to join her, and contribute of her experience to that meeting — such things need thinking about and praying over — but so interested that her face flushed at the thought that this girl, who was from the country, had more moral courage than she, and was in sympathy with Dr. Dennis' advanced ideas in regard to prayer-meetings.

As for Ruth Erskine, her head went down on the seat before her, and she kept it bowed during the remainder of the service.

Judge Burnham's nerves were in turmoil. He could not remember that he had ever in his life before felt such sympathy for the trials of others. This particular form of the trial seemed dreadful to him. The idea that a girl of Ruth Erskine's refinement, and a man of her father's position, should be brought thus rudely and offensively before the public, jarred upon him, as he had not supposed that anything outside of himself and his own trials could. He blamed himself for being the unwitting cause of part of the trouble. If he had not suggested to Ruth the possibility of coming to this obnoxious place, she would have been spared this embarrassment

Filling his mind with these thoughts — to the exclusion of anything else that was said — and trying to determine how he should best express his sympathy to this tried girl by his side, he was presently relieved to discover that the people were rising for the benediction, and this — to him — long drawn out trial was over. He had not, however, sufficiently composed his thoughts to venture on any form of address, when Ruth suddenly broke the silence in which they were walking:

"Judge Burnham, I owe you thanks. Your suggestion about the prayer-meeting to-night, and your kind attendance upon me, have helped. That meeting came to my heart like balm. I cannot venture to attempt telling you what it has done for me. Perhaps it would be difficult to make you understand how heavy my heart was; but one sentence spoken there has been repeated to me as a revelation! I am so glad to feel that, for *me*, there can be peace with God! I have felt so storm-tossed, so bewildered, so anxious to do right, and so sure that I was doing wrong, it has been, at times, difficult for me to determine right *from* wrong, and, in some things,

I have felt so condemned that I was miserable Now I know what I need — God's peace — such as only he can give — such as is not interfered with by any outward circumstances. To be justified *before him* is surely enough. I need not ask for further justification."

Now, indeed, was Judge Burnham silent from very amazement. Here was this girl, to whom he thought had come an added and excessively embarrassing trial, thanking him for bringing her into it, and actually calling it a help and a joy! He had not the least conception of what she could mean. A strong desire to make her explain herself, if she could, prompted his words:

"Then you were not disturbed with your — with the lady's prominence this evening?"

"With my sister's, Judge Burnham. You were right in the first place."

Whether Ruth was willing to accept the situation for herself or not, she could dignifiedly insist upon others doing it. Whoever her father introduced as his daughter should be received by *outsiders* as *her* sister, whether *she* so received her or not.

"I beg pardon," said Judge Burnham. "You were not disturbed, then, by the position which your sister took?"

"I didn't think anything about *position*. She recited that Bible verse most exquisitely, I thought, and the words which she spoke afterward were strong and helpful; they helped me, and I am glad in my very soul that I heard them. That is the most that I can tell you about it."

Silence seemed to be the wisest course for Judge Burnham. He was thrown out of his bearings. Since she did not need comfort, and refused to receive, why should he attempt to give it? But he didn't in the least understand her. He wondered curiously whether his sympathy had been equally thrown away on his friend, Judge Erskine, or whether he, with his refined and sensitive tastes, had really received a blow from which it would be hard to rally. The more he thought about it the more probable this seemed. As he thought he waxed indignant.

"If I were he I would forbid her appearance in public, until she learns what is due to her position. It isn't likely that he can rise to the fanatical heights where his daughter has managed to climb. Probably she will have made a descent by to-morrow morning. I mean to go in and see the Judge."

Acting upon this mental conclusion, he ascended the Erskine steps, and followed Ruth without waiting for a formal invitation. Her father had just entered, and was still in the hall. He turned toward his friend.

"Come in, Burnham. I was very glad to see you where I did to-night. I hope it will not be the last time. I am sure you must have enjoyed the meeting. Come to the library and let us talk it over." And Judge Erskine threw open the library door, while the others of his family turned toward the parlor.

"Well," he said, as the door closed after them, "what did you think of the meeting?"

"I confess to being considerably surprised," Judge Burnham answered. Truth to tell, he hadn't the least idea what it would be wise to say.

"Weren't you!" said Judge Erskine, with energy. "I never was more so. I didn't know she was of that stamp; and yet I might have known it. She has given me several glimpses of her spirit during the little time in which I have known anything about her."

"What are you going to do?"

"Do? How? I am not sure that I understand the question."

"Why, I mean as to the position which she assumed to-night."

"Oh, as to that, there is nothing to do. I dare say I may express the gratitude which I feel for the help that she gave me, but I don't even know whether I can bring myself to do *that*. I can't get over the sense of strangeness and embarrassment. But weren't those grand words that she quoted to-night? I declare such a truth as that ought to take us through anything! It lifts me out of myself for the time-being and I feel as though I could live my life patiently and earnestly. I'll tell you, Judge, what I thought as I sat in that seat to-night and looked over at you. I wished with all my soul that you might be induced to look into this matter for yourself, and see the reasonableness of it all. Did you ever give it special attention, my friend? In fact, I know you didn't, because a man of your discernment could have come to but one conclusion, had you thought closely about it."

"That is a compliment to my discernment, and I appreciate it," Judge Burnham said, with a faint attempt at a smile. "I am not sure that I ever gave the subject what you call 'special attention.' And yet I think I have a reasonable degree of respect for religion and the Bible. You have often heard me express my opinion of the literary merits of that book, I think."

"Oh, yes," said Judge Esrkine, with a little sigh. "'Literary merits!' Yes, I know you respect the Bible and admire it, and all that sort of thing; but that is very different from living by it. I respected it myself for forty years. The thing is to stand 'justified' in God's sight. Think of that! People like you and me, who have made mistakes all our lives — mistakes that seem past all rectifying — and yet, in God's sight, they are as if they had not been, through the atoning blood! Isn't that a glorious thought?"

"Mistakes are not *sins*, Judge," his friend added, and he spoke the words somewhat haughtily. In his heart he added: "They are a couple of fanatics, he and his daughter. I don't understand either of them." In truth, he was staggered. It might do to attribute fanaticism, or undue exaltation of mood, to Miss Erskine, possibly; but he had known the cool-headed Judge long and well. Was it likely that anything which would not bear close and logical looking into could get possession of him to a degree that it had — even to a degree that was transforming his life?

CHAPTER VII.

ONE DROP OF OIL.

NOW you know that some of you are anxious to hear all about that marriage which took place in the First Church, the next evening. You want to be told how the bride was dressed, and whether she had any bridesmaids, and whether Dr. Dennis appeared well, and how Grace Dennis was dressed, and how she acted, and who performed the ceremony, and whether it was a lengthy one, and every little detail of the whole matter; also, you are desirous of knowing how the "little gathering" that the Erskines gave, soon after, was managed — whether Mrs. Erskine became reconciled to the "black silk" and the "lace bow;" whether Susan proved to be yielding, or obstinate, and how Ruth bore up under the numerous petty embarrassments, which you plainly foresee the evening had in store for her. But, then, there are those discerning and sympathetic beings—the critics—standing all ready to pronounce on us, and say, that we are "prolix" and "commonplace" and "tedious;" that we spend too much time in telling about trivialities, and do not give the startling points fast enough, as if that were not exactly what we and they are doing all the time! Who lives exclamation points every day? There comes occasionally one into most lives (and assuredly Ruth Erskine believed that hers had come to her); but, for the most part, lives are made up of commas and interrogations and dashes. There is this comfort about professional critics — those that live behind the scenes know that when they are particularly hard on a book, one of two things is the case — either they have been touched in a sensitive spot by some of the characters delineated or opinions expressed, or else they have an attack of indigestion, and the first subject that comes under their dissecting

knives must bear the savage consequences. **Very
well,** let us give them a touch of "trivialities."
The bride's dress was a soft sheeny grey, just the
sort of dress for enduring a long, westward-bound
journey, and yet rich enough, and soft enough,
and delicate enough to look appropriate in the
church. As for Dr. Dennis. There is this satisfaction about a man's dress, it is easy of description. When you have said it was black, and
neat-fitting, what is there left to say? Some gentlemen look exceedingly well dressed, and some
look ungainly; and every one of them may have
on black clothes, that look to the uninitiated as
though they were well-fitted. What makes the
difference? What lady can tell?

The bright-eyed, fair-faced daughter of the
house of Dennis was really the beauty of that
evening; and, if the truth were known, the
bride-elect had expended more thought and care
upon the details of this young girl's attire than
she had on her own. Eurie Mitchell and Mr. Harrison were bridesmaid and groomsman. There
were those in the church who wondered at that,
and thought that Mr. Harrison would have liked
some one better than "that Mitchell girl" with

him, under the circumstances. But Eurie herself, and you and I, know better. We know he has chosen her, from all others, to stand by him forever.

After all, I can tell you nothing but the commonplaces. Is there ever anything else told about weddings? Who is able to put on paper the heart-throbs and the solemnities of such an hour? It is like all other things in life — that which is told is the least important of all the story.

Old Dr. Armington, whose hair was white with the snows of more than seventy winters, spoke the solemn words that made them man and wife... For half a century he had been, from time to time, repeating that solemn sentence.

"You are the two hundred and ninety-seventh couple that I have, in the name of my Master, joined for life. God bless you."

This was his low-spoken word to Dr. and Mrs. Dennis, as he took their hands in after greeting. Someway, it made Marion feel more solemn than before. Two hundred and ninety-six brides! She seemed to see the long procession filing past.

She wondered where they all were, and what had been their life-histories. Later in the evening, she could not resist the temptation to ask him, further:

"How many of the two hundred and ninety-six have you buried, Dr. Armington?"

And the old man's lip trembled, and his voice was husky, as he said:

"Don't ask me, child. A long array of names, among them two of my own daughters. But I shall sit down with a great many of them soon, at 'the marriage supper of the Lamb.' I hope none of them will wear starless crowns."

And Marion turned from him quickly, feeling that she had gotten her word to live by.

About that party. They lived through it, and, in a sense, it was a success. There were, of course, many mortifications; but by dint of shutting her eyes and her ears as far as possible, and keeping on the alert in every direction, and remembering her recent resolutions, very solemnly renewed, Ruth bore the ordeal reasonably well. She had more help than she knew of. Susan Erskine had inherited more of her father's nature than her mother's. It was not easy for her to yield, and she did not enjoy being managed. She could sacrifice her will, or her plans, or her comfort, if she saw a *need-be* for it, or if, in any sense, the strong, and, to her, solemn word, "Duty," could be put in as a plea; but to be controlled in the mere matter of her dress — and that, after she had determined that to spend time and money, other than was absolutely necessary, on the adorning of the perishing body, was a moral wrong — was something that could not be expected of her. She was not conscious of any other feeling than that of duty; but, in her heart, she was grieved, not to say insulted. Here had they — her mother and herself — been ignored for eighteen years, allowed to dress as they pleased, and go where they pleased, or not go at all; and, now that their tardy rights were being in a degree recognized, it was the paltry question of *dress* that must absorb them! She was willing to make many concessions to Ruth. There were times when she pitied her. In fact, she had constant and sincere sympathy for her in this invasion of home and name. She realized that the blame was in no sense Ruth's, and to shield her, as much as possible, from the inevitable suffering, was Susan's natural feeling. But, when it came to strictly personal questions — what colors she should wear, and what material, and how it should be made up — she rebelled. Surely those were matters which she had a right to decide for herself. Mother might be easily managed, if she would; perhaps it was well that she could be. But, for herself, Susan felt that it would be impossible, and hoped most earnestly that no attempt would be made in that direction.

As for Ruth, she thought of the matter in a troubled way, and shrank from entering into detail. The most she had done was to ask, hesitatingly, what she — Susan — would wear, on the evening in question. And Susan had answered her, coldly, that she "had not given the matter a thought, as yet." She supposed it would be time enough to think about that when the hour for dressing arrived. In her heart she knew that she had but one thing to wear; and Ruth knew it too, and knew that it was ill-chosen and ill-made, and in every way inappropriate. Yet she actually turned away, feeling unable to cope with the coldness and the evident reserve of this young woman over whom she could not hope to have influence.

Curiously enough, it was gentle little Flossy who stepped into these troubled waters, and poured her noiseless drop of oil. She came in the morning, waiting for Ruth to go with her to make a farewell call on Marion Wilbur, the morning before the wedding; and in the library, among the plants, giving them loving little touches here and there, was Susan.

"What is Marion to wear for travelling, do you know!" Flossy had asked of Ruth, as some word about the journey suggested the thought. And Ruth had answered briefly, almost savagely:

"I don't know. It is a blessed thing that no one will have to give it a thought. Marion will be sure to choose the most appropriate thing, and to have every detail in exquisite keeping with it. It is only lately that I have realized what a gift she had in that direction."

Then Ruth had gone away to make ready, and wise little Flossy, looking after her with the far-away, thoughtful look in her soft eyes, began to see one of her annoyances plainly, and to wonder if there were any way of helping. Then she went down the long room to Susan, busy among the plants.

"How pretty they are!" she said, sweetly. "What gorgeous coloring, and delicate tracery in the leaves! Does it ever occur to you to wonder that such great skill should have been expended in just making them look pretty to please our eyes?"

"No," said Susan, earnest and honest, "I don't think I ever thought of it."

"I do often. Just think of that ivy, it would have grown as rapidly and been quite as healthy if the leaves had been square, and all of them an intense green, instead of being shaded into that lovely dark, scolloped border all around the outer edge. 'He has made every thing beautiful in his time.' I found that verse one day last week, and I liked it *so much*. Since then I seem to be noticing everybody and everything, to see whether the beauty remains. I find it everywhere."

All this was wonderfully new to Susan Erskine. She was silent and thoughtful. Presently she said, "It doesn't apply to human beings — at least to many it doesn't. I know good men and women who are not beautiful at all."

"Wouldn't that depend a little on what one meant by beauty?" Flossy said, timidly. Argument was not her forte. "And then, you know, He *made* the plants and flowers — created their beauty for them, I mean, because they are soulless things — I think he left to us who are immortal, a great deal of the fashioning to do for ourselves."

"Oh, of course, there is a moral beauty which we find in the faces of the most ordinary, but I was speaking of physical beauty."

"So was I," said Flossy, with an emphatic nod of her pretty little head. "I didn't mean anything deep and wise, at all. I don't know anything about what they call 'esthetics,' or any of those scientific phrases. I mean just pretty things. Now, to show you how simple my thought was, that ivy leaf made me think of a pretty dress, well made and shapely, you know, and fitted to the face and form of the wearer. I thought the One who made such lovely plants, and finished them so exquisitely, must be pleased to see us study enough of His works to make ourselves look pleasing to the eyes of others."

Susan Erskine turned quite away from the plants and stared at her guest with wide, open, amazed eyes, for a full minute. "Don't you think," she asked at last, and her tone was of that stamp which indicates suppressed force — "don't you think that a great deal of time, and a great deal of money, and a great deal of force, which might do wonders elsewhere, are wasted on dress?"

"Yes," said Flossy, simply and sweetly, "I know that is so. After I was converted, for a little while it troubled me very much. I had been in the habit of spending a great deal of time and not a little money in that way, and I knew it must be wrong, and I was greatly in danger of going to the other extreme. I think for a few days I made myself positively ugly to my father and mother, by the unbecoming way in which I thought I ought to dress. But after awhile it came to me, that it really took very little more time to look *well* than it did to look ill-dressed; and that if certain colors became the form and complexion that God had given me, and certain others did not, there could be no religion in wearing those not fitted to me. God made them all, and he must have meant some of them specially for me, just as he specially thought about me in other matters. Oh, I haven't gone into the question very deeply; I want to understand it better. I am going to ask Mr. Roberts about it the very next time he comes. But, meantime, I feel sure that the Lord Jesus wants me to please my parents and my sister in every reasonable way. Sister Kitty is really uncomfortable if colors don't assimilate, and what right have I to make her uncomfortable, so long as the very rose leaves are tinted with just the color of all others that seemed fitted to them?"

Susan mused.

"What would you do," she asked presently, "if you had been made with that sense of the fitness of things left out? I mean, suppose you hadn't the least idea whether you ought to wear green, or yellow, or what. Some people are so constituted that they don't know what you mean when you tell them that certain colors don't assimilate; what are *they* to do?"

"Yes," said Flossy, gently and sweetly, "I

know what you mean, because people are made very differently about these things. I am trying to learn how to make bread. I don't know in the least. I can make cake, and desserts, and all those things, but Mr. Roberts likes the bread that our cook makes, and as I don't know how to make that kind, nor any other, I thought I ought to learn. It isn't a bit natural to me. I have to be very particular to remember all the tiresome things about it; I hadn't an idea there were so many. And I say to the cook, 'Now, Katy, what am I to do next? this doesn't look right at all.' And she comes and looks over my shoulder, and says, 'Why, child, you need more flour; always put in flour till you get rid of that dreadful stickiness.' Then I say to myself, 'That dreadful stickiness is to be gotten rid of, and flour will rid me of it, it seems,' and I determine in my own mind that I will remember that item for future use. I don't really like the work at all. It almost seems as though bread ought to be made without such an expenditure of time and strength. But it isn't, you know, and so I try; and when I think of how Mr. Roberts likes it, I feel glad that I am taking time and pains to learn. You know there are so many things to remember about it, from the first spoonful of yeast, down to the dampening of the crust and tucking up the loaves when they come out of the oven, that it really takes a good deal of memory. I asked Mr. Roberts once if he thought there would be any impropriety in my asking for ability to take in all the details that I was trying to learn. He laughed at me a little — he often does — but he said there could be no impropriety in praying about anything that it was proper to do."

"Thank you," said Susan Erskine, promptly. Then she did what was an unusual thing for her to do. She came over to the daintily dressed little blossom on the sofa, and bending her tall form, kissed the delicately flushed cheek, lightly and tenderly.

"Ruth," said little Flossy, as they made their way toward the street-car. "I think I like your new sister very much, indeed. I am not sure but she is going to be a splendid woman. I think she has it in her to be grandly good."

"When did you become such a discerner of character, little girlie?" was Ruth's answer, but she felt grateful to Flossy. The words had helped her.

As for Susan, she went back to the plants, and hovered over them quite as lovingly, but more thoughtfully than before. She studied the delicately-veined leaves and delicately-tinted blossoms all the while, with a new light in her eyes. This small sweet-faced girl, who had looked to the plainly-attired, narrow-visioned Susan, like a carefully prepared edition of a late fashion-plate, had given her some entirely new ideas in regard to this question of dress. It seemed that there was a *duty* side to it that she had not canvassed. "What right have I to make her uncomfortable?" gentle Flossy had asked, speaking of her sister Kitty. Susan repeated the sentence to herself, substituting Ruth's name for Kitty's. Presently she went to her own room.

"Ruth," she said, later in the day, when they were for a moment alone together "would you like to have me get a new dress for the tea-party?"

Tea-party was a new name for the social gathering, but it was what Susan had heard such gatherings called. Ruth hesitated, looked at the questioner doubtfully a moment, then realizing that here was one with whom she could be straightforward, said frankly, "Yes, I would, very much."

"What would you like me to get?"

"I think you would look well in one of those dark greens that are almost like an ivy-leaf in tint. Do you know what I mean?"

Susan laughed. She did not take in the question; she was thinking that it was a singular and a rather pleasant coincidence that she should be advised to dress after the fashion of the ivy-leaf which had served for illustration in the morning.

"I don't suppose I ever looked well in my life," she said at last, smiling brightly. "Perhaps it would be well to try the sensation. If you will be so kind, I should like you to select and purchase a dress for me that shall be according to your taste, only remembering that I dress as plainly as is consistent with circumstances, from principle."

When she was alone again, she said, with an amused smile curving her lip, "I must get rid of that dreadful stickiness, and flour will do it!'

That is what the dear little thing said. "Dark green will do it for me, it seems. If I find that to be the case I must remember it."

Ruth dressed for shopping with a relieved heart. She was one of those to whom shopping was an artistic pleasure, besides she had never had anyone, save herself, on which to exhibit taste. She was not sure that it would be at all disagreeable.

"She begins to comprehend the necessities of the position a little, I believe," she said, meaning Susan. And *she* didn't know that Flossy Shipley's gentle little voice, and carefully chosen words, had laid down a solid plank of *duty* for her uncompromising sister to tread upon.

CHAPTER VIII.

FINDING ONE'S CALLING.

DURING the days which preceded that social gathering, Ruth found her mind often busy with the wonders of the verse which had been quoted at prayer-meeting. She recognized it as from the chapter which she had read in the morning, and she re-read it, filled with a new sense of its meaning. She sought after and earnestly desired to realize peace with God. How wonderful would it be to be able to say, "And not only so, but we glory in tribulation!" Poor Ruth believed that she understood the meaning of that word, "tribulation." Would it be possible for her ever to "glory" in it? As she read those verses and thought about them, she seemed to hear again the peculiar ring of triumph that there was in Susan's voice, as she repeated the words, "*She* feels it." Ruth said to herself, "I believe she knows more about these things than I do; I wonder how she came to get the thought in the first place? I read the verse and didn't take it in. Perhaps she has taken in other things, about which I know nothing, and which would help me?"

Thinking these thoughts, dwelling on them, they culminated in a sudden resolution, which led her to tap at the door of Susan's room. She was cordially invited to enter. Susan was engaged in dusting the row of books, in dull and somewhat shabby binding, that ornamented the pretty table under the gaslight.

"Have a seat," she said; "I can't think how the dust gets at my books so often; I put them in order this morning. They are my good old friends, and I like to take special care of them, but they are fading."

She fingered the bindings with loving hands, and Ruth, curious to see what they were, drew near enough to read some of the titles, "Cruden's

Concordance," "A Bible Text-Book," "Barnes Notes on the Gospels," and "Bushnell's Moral Uses of Dark Things." The others were old and, some of them, obsolete school text-books.

"I haven't many," Susan said, in a tender tone, "but they are very useful. They have been my best friends for so long that I think I should be a real mourner over the loss of one of them."

The new dark-green dress lay on the bed, and some soft, rare laces, a gift to Susan that day from her father, lay beside it. Ruth glanced that way, "Have you tried on the dress since it was finished?"

"No, I thought it would be time enough in the morning, and I had a little reading that I was anxious to do this evening."

"What are you reading? something that you like?"

"Yes, very much," Susan said, with a rare smile lighting her pale face; "I only began it the other night. I didn't know it was so rich. It is the first chapter of Colossians, but I only read to the fifth verse."

Ruth looked her amazement. "Why, you

must have been interrupted very constantly."

Susan shook her head. "No, on the contrary, I spent very nearly an hour over those four verses; the longer I studied on them the more remarkable they became, and I found myself held."

"Is the meaning so very obscure?"

"Not at all; the meaning is there on the surface; the only thing is, there is so much, and it leads one's thoughts in so many different ways. Do you remember the second verse?"

"I don't remember it at all; very likely I never read it."

"Well, the second verse is addressed, 'To the saints and faithful brethren in Christ, which are at Colosse.' That sentence arrested my thoughts completely. Suppose I had been living at Colosse in those days, could I have claimed that letter to the *saints?* I stopped over the word and wondered over it, and queried just what it meant, and it meant so much that I should really have gotten no farther than that sentence if I had not deliberately left it and gone on to the 'Grace be unto you and peace.' I found my heart craving peace: I think I was somewhat like the child who claims the reward, or reaches out after it, without waiting to be sure whether he has met the conditions."

"But I don't understand you very well What about saints? they were holy men, were they not, set apart for special work at that special time? How *could* their experience touch yours?"

"I don't think so. I think they were just men and women who loved the Lord Jesus Christ, and were called by his name, just as you and I are."

"But *we* are not saints; at least I am not."

"But you are called to be?"

"I don't understand you."

"*Don't* you? Think of that verse of Paul's, 'Unto the Church of God, which is at Corinth, to them that are sanctified in Christ Jesus, *called to be saints.*' Now, you know *we* are sanctified in Christ Jesus, so are we not called to be saints?"

"I don't know what 'sanctified' means very well; and, besides, I can't help thinking that the letter was written to the Church at Corinth. *I* don't live in Corinth; how do I know that the address fits me? If I should find a letter addressed to the people who live on Twenty-third Street, wouldn't I be likely to say, 'Well, I have nothing to do with that; I live on Fifth Avenue?'"

"Ah! but suppose the very next sentence read, 'And to all that love the Lord Jesus Christ,' wouldn't you claim the letter?"

"Yes," said Ruth, with a flash of joy in her face, "I think I could."

"Well, don't you know the next words are, 'With all that in every place call upon the name of Jesus Christ our Lord, both theirs and ours.'"

"I never thought of it," said Ruth. Then, after a little, "Did you find out what a saint was?"

"Why I found some characteristics of them, and tried to see if they answered my description. Have you ever looked the matter up?"

"No," said Ruth, "I did not so much as know that I was expected to be a saint; tell me what you found."

"Why," said Susan, drawing her chair and opening her Bible, "see here, I found a promise, 'He will keep the feet of his saints.' It made me all the more eager to learn as to my claim. Was I his saint? would he keep me? In that same verse there is a contrast, 'He will keep the feet of his saints, and the wicked shall be silent in darkness.' Now, if there are only two classes of people, saints and the wicked, which am I? In God's sight who are the wicked? I looked for a description of them and found this statement: 'The Lord preserveth all them that love him, but all the wicked will he destroy.' Now, I *know* I love the Lord, and I know that he will not destroy me, for I have in my heart the assurance of his promise. If that is so, *I* must be one of his saints. Then I found the promise, 'He shall give his angels charge over thee, to keep thee in all thy ways.' Keep who? And looking back a little I found, 'He that dwelleth in the secret place of the Most High shall abide under the shadow of the Almighty. But he promises to keep only those who are *his saints*. Then I found the promise, 'He maketh intercession for the *saints*.' Now, I said, if there is no one interceding between a just God and me, what will become of me? But I found the inspired statement of St. Paul, 'Wherefore he is able to save them to the uttermost that come unto God by him, seeing he ever liveth to make intercession for *them*.' That puts me at once among those for whom he intercedes, and his special work in heaven is to make intercession for the saints. By this time I was ready to claim the name, and you may know I was anxious to find what it meant. I went to the dictionary; the first definition I found was, 'A person sanctified.' That startled me. Could it be that I was sanctified? Why, I feel so sinful, and so weak, and so small! Well, I said, What does 'sanctified' mean? and I found that it was defined as set apart to a holy or religious use. It recalled to my mind the statement of Paul, 'But ye are washed, but ye are sanctified, but ye are justified in the name of the Lord Jesus.' A great deal ought to be expected of us, after that."

Ruth drew a long sigh. "I don't know anything about it, I believe," she said, sadly; "I never read the Bible in that way. Half the time it doesn't seem to have anything in it really for me."

"Don't you think that some of our trouble is

in being content with simply *reading*, not *studying* the Bible? I thought the other night that if I had spent an hour on geometry, and then begun to understand it somewhat, I should feel as though I were repaid. But sometimes I read a Bible verse over two or three times, and then, because its meaning is obscure, I feel half discouraged. I was speaking of it to — to father last evening, and he said he thought the trouble was largely in that direction." Susan had not yet gotten so that she could speak the unfamiliar name without hesitation. As for Ruth, her brow clouded; it did not seem to her that she could ever share that name with anyone. But she was interested — and deeply so — in the train of thought which had been started.

"What next?" she asked, curious to see whither Susan's thoughts had led her. "You said you read no farther than the fourth verse. What stopped you there? I don't see much in it;" and she leaned forward and re-read the verse from Susan's open Bible.

"Oh, why *don't* you? 'Since we heard of your faith in Christ Jesus, and of the love which ye have to all the saints.' That verse stopped me longer than any other, especially the sentence: 'Since we heard of your faith in Christ Jesus'—it is such a common form of expression. I thought of it last evening while listening to the talk in the parlor. 'I heard that the Wheelers were going abroad,' some one said; and another, 'I heard that Dr. Thomas was soon to bring a wife home.' Two of the young ladies talked in low tones, and nearly all I could catch was the expression: 'I heard he was,' or 'she was,' or 'they were.' It was evident that a great deal had been heard about a great many people. I said over the verse: 'We heard of your faith in Christ Jesus.' Who hears of such things? How many people have such marked and abiding faith in Christ Jesus, that when we talk of them we say, 'I heard that Miss So and So had the most implicit faith in the power of Christ to keep her.' Now wouldn't that be a strange thing to say?"

"I should think it would," said Ruth, amazed at this train of thought. "After all, I suppose many people have the *faith;* only it is not the custom in society to talk about such things'

"I don't," answered Susan, positively. "Of

course many people have it in a degree; but not to such an extent that it arouses interest, and excites remark. I think it is the custom in society to talk about that which interests people — which has been suggested to their minds by passing events. I have heard that it is a very common thing in localities where Mr. Moody has been holding meetings, to discuss his remarkable faith and love. Don't you suppose, if my Christian life were so marked a force that all who came in contact with me, felt its influence, it would be natural to speak of it, when my friends chanced to mention my name?"

"I suppose so," Ruth said, slowly. "At least I don't see why it should not be; and, indeed, it is very common for people to talk about the change in Flossy Shipley."

Susan's voice was very earnest. "I wish I could bear such testimony as that. I believe it would be right to be ambitious in that direction; to live so that when people spoke of me at all, the most marked thing they could say about me would be, not, how I dressed, or appeared, or talked, but how strong my faith in the Lord Jesus was, and how it colored all my words and acts. Wouldn't that be a grand ambition?"

"And of the love which ye have to all the saints," Ruth repeated, half aloud, half to herself; her eye had caught the words again. Suddenly she started, and the blood flowed in ready waves into her cheeks. She had caught a new and personal meaning to the words — "love to *all* the saints." Suppose this usurper of home and name, who sat near her — this objectionable sister — suppose *she* were one of the saints! — and I verily believe she is, Ruth said to her beating heart — then, would it be possible so to live, that people would ever say, "She loves that sister of her's, because she recognizes in her one of the Lord's own saints?" Nothing looked less probable than this! She could not bring her heart to feel that she could *ever* love her. A sort of kindly interest, she might grow to feel, an endurance that would become passive, and, in a sense, tolerable, but could she ever help paling, or flushing, when she heard this new voice say "father," and realized that she had a right to the name, even as she herself had? She had been the only Miss Erskine so long; and she had been so proud of the old aristocratic name, and she had felt so deeply the blot upon its honor, that it seemed to her she could never come to look with anything like *love* upon one connected with the bitterness. Yet, it did flash over her, with a strange new sense of power, that Susan Erskine held nearer relation to her than even these human ties. If *she* was indeed a daughter of the Most High, if the Lord Jesus Christ was her Elder Brother, then was this girl her sister, a daughter of royal blood, and perhaps — she almost believed it — holding high position up there, where souls are looked at, instead of bodies.

A dozen times, during the evening which followed this conversation, did the words of this Bible verse, and the thoughts connected therewith, flash over Ruth. It was the evening of the social gathering. Now, that Susan had called her attention to it, she was astonished over the number of times that those words: "I heard," were on people's lips. They had heard of contemplated journeys, and changes in business, and changes in name, and reverses, and good fortunes, and contemplated arrangements for amusement, or entertainment, or instruction; *everything* they had heard about their friends or their acquaintances. Yet, no one said, during the whole evening — so far as she knew — that they had heard anything very marked about the religious life of anyone. In fact, religious life was one of the things that was not talked of at all; so Ruth thought. If she had stood near Judge Burnham and her sister, at one time, she would have heard him saying:

"He is a man of mark in town; one prominent on every good occasion; noted for his philanthropy and generosity, and is one of the few men whom everybody seems to trust, without ever having their confidence jarred. I have heard it said, that his word would be taken in any business transaction as quickly as his bond would be."

"Is he a Christian man?" Susan had asked; and a half-amused, half-puzzled look had shadowed Judge Burnham's face, as he answered: "As to that, I really don't know. I have never heard that he made any professions in that direction, though it is possible that he may be connected with some church. Why, Miss Erskine, do you think it impossible for a man to be honest and honorable and philanthropic, unless he has made some profession of it in a church?"

Then Susan had looked at the questioner steadily and thoughtfully a moment before she answered: "I was not thinking of possible morality; I was simply wondering whether the man who was building so fair and strong a house had looked to it, that it was founded upon a rock, or whether he really were so strangely improvident as to build upon the sand. You know *I* think, that, 'other foundation can no man lay than that which is laid, Jesus Christ being the chief corner-stone.'"

So there was some religious conversation at the Erskines' party, and it sent Judge Burnham home thinking. And now, though the fruits of that evening's gathering will go on growing and ripening and being gathered in, from human lives, so far as we personally are concerned, we are done with that party.

CHAPTER IX.

A SOCIETY CROSS.

THE next thing that occurred to mar the peace of this much-tried young lady — she went out calling with her step-mother. This duty was passed over just as long as it would do to ignore the claims of society, she being finally driven to it by realizing that more talk was being made by *not* going than would be likely to result from going. Then, with foreboding heart, she made ready. She planned at first to escape it all and have her father the victim. But there were two difficulties. He had rarely made other than professional calls, or most ceremonious ones on persons high in the profession, and, therefore this whole matter would be so new to him that to tide the bewildered wife through it would be well-nigh impossible. And, besides, Ruth felt the necessity of being present, to know the very worst that could be said or done, and to attempt going as a trio was not to be thought of for a moment. There was one bright spot in her annoyances: It was pleasant to remember the look of relief which gleamed over her father's face when she told him he could be excused from attendance on them if he chose. "I can save him *so* much, at least," she told herself, and it helped her to make ready. "If she would *only* keep perfectly quiet!" she murmured again to herself, as she waited at the door of her mother's room for the last glove to be drawn on, and marked what an effect the rich black silk, with its perfect fitting seams, and perfectly draped folds had on the dumpy figure. "If she only *could* get along without talking she would do very well."

Great attention had been paid by Ruth to the details of this toilet. The soft laces at throat and wrist, the rich mantle, the shapely hat with the unmistakable air of "style" about it, even to the gloves of exactly the right shade and size, had each been objects of separate study; and Mrs. Erskine, though occasionally she had fond memories of the green silk dress, and the red bow — which she began to be dimly conscious were never destined to shine together — yet took in so much of the general effect as filled her with surprise and reconciled her to the position of lay figure in Ruth's hands, looking upon her step-daughter with the same degree of surprised awe that a statue might, could it be gifted with life and behold itself getting draped for the tableau.

The calls started nicely, Flossy Shipley's being the first home at which they halted. Flossy, in her sweet, winning, indescribable way, decoyed Mrs. Erskine into a corner easy chair, and engaged her in low-toned, earnest, even absorbed conversation, while Ruth tried to unbend from her dignity and chat with Flossy's cheery, social mother. Glancing from time to time toward the elder woman and the fair young girl, and noting the fact that both were unmistakably interested in their subject for conversation, Ruth found herself wondering what it *could* be. Whatever it was she was grateful, and gave Flossy a most informal and tender kiss at parting, by way of expressing her relief.

Then, too, Dr. and Mrs. Dennis were at home, and were joyfully glad to see them, and Dr. Dennis held Mrs. Erskine's attention, leaving Ruth free to talk with, and look at, and wonder over Marion, she seemed so fresh and bright and glad; full of eagerness, full of plans, full of heartiness, for any and everything that might be mentioned. "She is at least ten years younger than I ever knew her to be," was Ruth's mental conclusion as she watched the expressive face. There was no restraint in their talk. Ruth felt, that for the time-being, she could throw off the burden of responsibility and have a good time. She did not know what Dr. Dennis was saying to her step-mother, and she did not care, it was so pleasant to feel that she could trust him, that he was a friend, and would neither repeat to others the mistakes of the uncultured woman with whom he talked, nor laugh about them with Marion when she was gone. Ruth not only respected and liked, but thoroughly trusted her pastor.

"I am glad she married him," she told herself, glancing from one to the other, and feeling, rather than noticing, that they were both evidently heartily glad about the same thing. "They are just exactly suited to each other, and that is saying a good deal for them both. What a blessed change the brightness of this room must be when she compares it with that little den of hers, up the third flight of stairs!" Yes, and there was another side to that. What a nameless charm, as of home, she had thrown over the propriety of the parsonage parlor! Before, it had been a *room*—pleasant and proper, and well-cared for, as became the parsonage parlor—now, it was *home!* Presently, too, came Gracie, with her beautiful face and gracious manner, free and cordial and at ease. "Mamma," she said as naturally as though it had been a name constantly on her lips; and, indeed, it was plain that she enjoyed the name. There were no sad contrasts to dim her eyes, or quicken the beatings of her heart, the real mother having only had time to give her darling one clinging kiss before God called her home. "She may well be proud of such a mother as her father has brought to *her*," Ruth thought, looking from one to the other, and noting the glance of sympathy which passed between them. And then she sighed, being drawn back to her heavier lot. Marion's dreary life had blossomed into brightness, while all that was ever bright had gone out of hers; at least so it seemed to her. Then she arose, realizing that nothing of this afternoon's crosses would be borne if she whiled the time on Flossy Shipley and Marion Dennis.

From the moment that the two were seated in Mrs. Schuyler Colman's parlor peace left Ruth's heart. Here was responsibility, solemn and overwhelming — how to tide this uncultured woman through the shoals and breakers of this aristocratic atmosphere. No sooner was Mrs. Erskine fairly seated than she broke the proprieties of the occasion with the exclamation:

"Why, my patience! if there isn't Dr. Mason Kent, staring right straight at me! What a splendid likeness! I declare I most feel as though he ought to speak to me."

"Was Dr. Kent an acquaintance of yours?"

Nothing could be colder, more lofty, more in keeping with the proprieties, than the tone in which Mrs. Schuyler Colman asked the question.

"An acquaintance! why I guess he was. I sewed in his house nigh on two months before his oldest daughter was married. They had a regular seamstress in the house, one who belonged to the family, you know. O! they were high up in the world, I tell you. But she needed extra help when the rush came, and there was always lots of plain sewing to do, anyway, and the woman I sewed for last recommended me, and I got in. It was a nice place. They gave good pay; better than I ever got anywhere else, and I always remembered Dr. Kent; he was as kind as he could be."

Shall I try to describe to you the glow on Ruth Erskine's face? What had become of her haughty indifference to other people's opinions? What had become of her loftily expressed scorn of persons who indulged in pride of station, or pride of birth? Ah! little this young woman knew about her own heart. Gradually she was discovering that *she* had plenty of pride of birth and station and name. The thing which had seemed plebeian to her was to *exhibit* such pride in a marked way before others.

Mrs. Colman seemed to consider it necessary to make some reply :

"Dr. Kent is an uncle of mine," she said, and her voice was freezing in its dignity.

"You don't say! Where is he now? How I should like to see the dear old man! I wonder, Ruth, that your pa didn't tell me his relatives lived here. It was at his house that I first saw your pa. I shall never forget that night, if I live to be a hundred. They had a party, or a dinner, or — well, I forget what the name of it was; but it was after the wedding, you know, and crowds of fashionables was there. I was in a back passage, helping sort out the rubbers and things that had got mixed up; and I peeked out to see them march to dinner; and I see them all as plain as day. I said then — says I, to Mirandy Bates, the girl that I was helping: "That tall man with the long whiskers and pale face is the stylishest one amongst 'em, I think." And who do you suppose it was but your pa! Land alive! I had just as much idea of marrying him, *then*, as I had of flying and no more."

"I should suppose so," said Mrs. Schuyler Colman. She could not resist the temptation o saying it, though Ruth darted a lightning glance at her from eyes that were gleaming in a face that had become very pale. She arose suddenly, remarking that they were making a very lengthy call; and Mrs. Erskine, to whom the call seemed very short, began to be uncomfortably conscious that she had been talking a great deal, and perhaps not to Ruth's liking. She relapsed into an embarrassed silence, and made her adieu in the most awkward manner possible. Had Ruth taken counsel of her own nerves, she would have felt it impossible to endure more, and have beaten a retreat; but to sustain her was the memory of the fact that certain calls *must* be made, and, that if she did not make them, her father must. When it came to the martyr spirit, and she could realize that she was being martyrized in her father's place, she could endure. But, oh, if she could *only* manage to give this dreadful woman a hint as to the proprieties! And yet, suppose she stopped that dreadful tide of reminiscences, what *would* the woman talk about? Still, at all hazards, it must be risked:

"I do not think," she began, in a tone so constrained that the very sound of it frightened her step-mother. "I do not think that my father would like to have you refer to your past life, among his friends."

"My patience!" said Mrs. Judge Erskine. "Why not? I never done anything to be ashamed of — never in my life. I was an honest, respectable girl. There ain't one who knew me but could tell you that; and, as to being poor, why, I couldn't help that, you know; and I ain't been rich such a dreadful long time that I've forgot how it felt, neither. Not that your pa kept me close; he never did that. But I kept myself close, you see, because I had no kind of a notion that he was so rich."

This was worse than the former strain. Ruth was almost desperate:

"It makes no difference to me how poor you were, Madam, but it is not the custom in society to tell all about one's private affairs."

And then, in the next breath, she wondered what Judge Erskine would have said, could he have heard her address his wife in that tone, and with those words. At least she had frightened her into silence. And they rang at Mrs. Huntington's and were admitted — an angry woman, with flashing eyes, and a cowed woman, who wished she was at home, and didn't know what to say. Poor Ruth was sorry that she had interfered. Perhaps any sort of talk would have been less observable that this awkward, half frightened silence; also, Judge Burnham was in the room, at the other end of the parlor, among the books, as one familiar there. Mrs. Huntington belonged to the profession. Was it more or less embarrassing because of his presence? Ruth could not bring herself to being sure which it was. Mrs. Huntington was a genial woman, though an exceedingly stylish one; but she knew as little how to put a frightened, constrained person at ease, as it was possible to know about anything; and yet her heart was good enough.

"I suppose you attended the concert, last evening, Mrs. Erskine?" she said, addressing that lady with a smile, and in a winning tone of voice. But Mrs. Erskine looked over at Ruth, in the absurd fashion of a naughty child, who, having been punished for some misdemeanor, glances at you, to be sure that he is not offending in the same way again. Ruth was selecting a card from her case to leave for Miss Almina Huntington, and apparently gave no notice to her mother. Left thus to her own resources, what could she do but answer, as best she knew how?

"Well, no, I didn't. Judge Erskine got tickets, and said he would take me if I wanted to go; but I didn't want to go. The fact is, I suppose, it is want of education, or something; but I ain't a might of taste for those concerts. I like singing, too. I used to go to singing-school, when I was a girl, and I was reckoned to have a good voice, and I used to like it first-rate — sang in the choir, you know, and all that; but these fiddle-dee-dee, screech-owl performances that they get off nowadays, and call music, I can't stand, nohow. I went to one of 'em. I thought I'd like to please Judge Erskine, you know, and I went; and they said it was fine, and perfectly glorious, and all that; but I didn't think so, and that's the whole of it. I gaped and gaped the whole blessed evening. I was ashamed of myself, but I couldn't help it. I tried to listen, too, and get the best of it, but it was just yelp and howl, and I couldn't make out a word, no more than if it had been in Dutch; and I dunno but it was. I don't like 'em, and I can't help it.'

Mrs. Erskine was growing independent and indignant. Silence was not her forte, and, in the few minutes which she had spent thus, she had resolved not to pretend to be what she wasn't.

"I don't like them yelping, half-dressed women, nor them roaring men," she said, swiftly, to herself, "and I mean to say so. Why shouldn't I?"

Poor Ruth! It was not that she enjoyed or admired operatic singing, or the usual style of modern concert singing. In a calm, dignified, haughty way, she had been heard to say that she thought music had degenerated, and was being put to very unintellectual uses in these days, in comparison with what had been its place. But that was such a very different thing from talking about "fiddle-dee-dee," and "screeching," and "howling," and, above all, "*gaping!*" What *could* be said? Mrs. Huntington was not equal to the occasion. She was no more capable of appreciating what there was of beauty in the singing than her caller was, but she was aware that society expected her to appreciate it;

so she did it! Judge Burnham came to the rescue:

"You are precisely of my mind, Mrs Erskine," he said, appearing from the recesses of the back parlor, and bowing to Ruth, while he advanced to offer his hand to her step-mother. "You have characterized the recent concerts in the exact language that they deserve. Such singing is not music; it is simply 'fiddle-dee-dee!'"

"Why, Judge Burnham!"

This, in an expostulating tone, from Mrs. Huntington.

"Fact, my dear Madam. It was simply screeching, last evening; nothing else in the world. I was a victim, and I defy anyone, with a cultured taste, to have enjoyed it. It was almost an impossibility to endure. Mrs. Erskine, I want to show you a picture, which I think you will like, if you will step this way with me."

And he escorted the gratified little woman down the length of the parlor, and devoted himself carefully to her, during the rest of the very brief call which Ruth made. He came, also, to the very door-steps with her, talking still to the mother, covering with dextrous gallantry her awkwardness of manner and movement.

"Thank you," said Ruth, in a low tone, as he turned to her with a parting bow. She could not help it, and she did not fail to notice the gleam of pleasure which lighted his grave face at her words.

"Aren't you tired?" she asked her mother, as they moved away from the Huntington mansion. Her martyr spirit had passed from her. She felt utterly worn, as if it were impossible for her to endure more. "Don't you want to go home?"

"Bless you, yes. I'm clear tuckered out. I didn't dream that it was such awful hard work to make calls. I don't wonder your pa didn't want to go. Yes, let's go home, for the land's sake!"

And they went home. When Ruth thought of Judge Burnham at all, during the next few days, it was with a sense of gratitude, which was new, and not unpleasant.

CHAPTER X.

OTHER PEOPLE'S CROSSES.

ONE could not live long in this world without realizing the forcefulness of the sentence: "Every heart knoweth his own bitterness." Behind the sunniest, apparently most enviable life the bitterness hides. It will not be supposed that Marion Dennis' life, which, to Ruth's narrow vision, had blossomed into perfect coloring, was an exception to the general rule.

As she stands in her pretty dining-room, waiting for the coming of her husband, and gazes out of the window at the play of light and shade in the western sky — gazes with that far-away, thoughtful, half-sad look, which betokens that the gazer's thoughts are not upon the picture which her eyes behold — it is plain, to the most careless glance, that a tinge of somber hue has already shaded the picture of her life. She had been through an ordeal of calls, that afternoon; not calls from intimate and congenial friends, who came because they desired the pleasure of a visit with her, but from some of those who came, as in custom bound, to pay a ceremonious visit to the new wife of their pastor. They had not been helpful callers. Without offending any of the set rules which are supposed to govern polite society, they had yet contrived to make Marion feel that they were keen-sighted, keen-scented society spies, with eyes all about them, and ears alert to hear, or to fancy what they could. Also, they had been people — some of them — who delighted in what they termed plain speaking, which is ofttimes decorous insult, if that expression is not a misnomer. There are people not quite coarse enough to express adverse criticism directly to a man's face, and such are apt to resort to the more refined coarseness of making their criticism into the form of a joke, and aiming it at the face of his wife! With one or two such persons had Marion come in contact.

"I hope you have Dr. Dennis in good subjection," Mrs. Easterly had said, with a peculiar little laugh that was meant to be merry, and that jarred, without one's being able to define why. "There is nothing like beginning right, you know. I told Mr. Easterly, last evening, I was afraid you would be too lenient with him; he is positively in danger of keeping us in prayer-meeting until it is time to be thinking about the next morning's breakfast! Mr. Easterly said, when he got him a wife, home would be more attractive to him; but my dear Mrs. Dennis, you must have observed that there was no improvement last evening."

"I observed that he was five minutes past the hour," Marion said; and, if Mrs. Easterly had been familiar with her voice, she would have discovered that it was haughty in the extreme. "Dr. Dennis is very particular to close promptly, and, when I questioned him, he said the people were tardy about getting in, and so delayed the opening."

"*Possible* that it was only five minutes! I could have been positive it was fifteen!" Mrs. Easterly said, ignoring the explanation, and the statement about general punctuality. Such people always ignore remarks that are not easy to be answered. Then the smooth voice went on: "I think a clergyman should try to cultivate habits of punctuality about *closing*, as well as opening meetings, so many people are overwearied by long drawn out exercises."

"As, for instance, lectures by infidels, and the like," remarks Marion, still with the dryness of tone that those familiar to her understand, and calling to mind the fact that she had heard of Mrs. Easterly as a delighted listener, for an hour and three quarters, to the popular infidel orator, two evenings before.

"Oh, *lectures!* Why, of course, they have a set time; every one knows they must be lengthy. They have abstruse themes to handle, and many classes of hearers to please."

"But the mere commonplaces of a prayer-meeting can be compressed into small compass, as well as not, the theme of personal salvation not being supposed to be of much importance, nor very abstruse, I suppose."

Mrs. Easterly arched her eyebrows; said nothing, because she didn't know what to say; made the rest of her stay brief, and remarked, when she had gotten out of Marion's hearing, that she had heard *that* Miss Wilbur spoken of as peculiar — having infidel tendencies, indeed. Perhaps there was a shade of truth in it. For her part, she wondered that Dr. Dennis should have been so imprudent as to have selected that sort of a wife. It was imprudent in Marion to have answered her caller in those words, or in that spirit. Sarcasm was lost on her, for she hadn't the right sort of brains to understand it. It is a curious fact that certain people, who can be very sarcastic in themselves, can not understand or appreciate it in others.

And so trivial a matter as this troubled Marion? Well, yes, it did. She had not been long in her position, you will remember. It was really her first rude awakening from the dream that all Christian people regarded their pastor with a certain reverent courtesy; not in a cringing or servile spirit, not in a spirit in any sense

at variance with true independence of thought
and action, but in the chivalrous spirit of the
olden time, reverencing the office, rather than
the man, and according all possible courtesy to
the man, *because* of the position he held, as
ambassador from the King's court. Marion's
early childhood had been spent among simple,
earnest Christians — Christians whose reverent
spirit had been an outgrowth of Puritan New
England; and, while her later years had passed
among a very different class of people, she yet
had clung to the fancy that *Christians* everywhere cherished the bond of relationship — the
tie stronger than that of blood — and spoke
wisely and with respect of those who belonged,
like themselves, to the royal family. Mrs. Easterly's words had jarred, not only because Dr.
Dennis was her husband, but because he was a
clergyman, and because he was Mrs. Easterly's
pastor. Much had she to learn, you will
observe! She was more than likely to meet
often with people to whom the word "pastor"
meant less than any other title — meant, if they
took time to analyze their own feelings, one to
whom they could be rude, or free, or insultingly

inquisitive, without fear of rousing him to resentment, because resentment is not a becoming trait in the ministry!

Dr. Dennis would have smiled could he have known the turmoil in his wife's heart. He had so long ago passed beyond that — had so long ago decided that people must be ranked in classes — so many from this strip of humanity, who did not know the difference between frankness and rudeness — so many in this strip, who, because of their lack of early education, must not be expected to know certain things — so many in this strip, to whom he could talk, freely, familiarly, as brother to brother, and friend to friend — classified Christians, belonging to the family, indeed, but having such different degrees of likeness to the family name that, what was a matter of course from one, was a sting from another. All these things Dr. Dennis knew; all these things his wife had still to learn. She was willing to learn, and she was not so foolish as to suppose that her road was strewn with roses; but, all the same, the tiny thorn pricked her.

There were other and graver troubles than this. Do you remember how she pleased her

nancy, while yet she was an inhabitant of that dingy third-story room, as to the dainty little teas she would get for that young daughter of hers? Here it was, the very perfection of a tea-table, exquisite and delicate and fascinating in all its appointments; laid for three, yet, presently, when Dr. Dennis came from his round of calls, and seated himself opposite his wife, and waited, and then finally sent a messenger to Gracie's room, who returned with the message, "Miss Grace says will you please excuse her this evening, she doesn't care for any tea," his face clouded, as though the answer brought trouble to his heart.

"Have you had further talk with Grace?" he asked his wife, when the door had closed on the servant.

"A little. There have been callers most of the time, but I talked with her a few minutes."

"What did she say?"

Marion would rather he had not asked the question. She hesitated a little, then said, with an effort to speak lightly:

"She said what was natural enough — that she thought *I* knew almost too much about the matter, and might have been content to leave it to you."

"I will not have her speaking in that manner to you," he said, his face growing graver, and his forehead settling into a frown. "She ought to know better."

"I know it," answered Marion, a little dash of brightness in her voice. "She ought to be perfect, of course, and not give way in this undignified manner. It is only such old saints as you and I who have any right to get out of tone, when things do not go just to suit us."

He laughed a little, then he said:

"Now, Marion, you know she has tried you very much, and without cause."

"As to that, I suppose if you and I could see into her heart, she thinks she has sore cause. I would not make too much of it, if I were you; and I would make nothing at all of the part which has to do with me. She will feel differently before very long. She is young."

Then Dr. Dennis' thoughts went back to his daughter. He sighed heavily:

"I ought to have shielded her better; I was trying, I thought. I am so astonished about that man! He has been a professor of religion ever since he was a child."

"To profess a thing is not always to possess it," Marion said, and then she sighed to think that even in religion this was so true; and she sighed again to realize that in her hard life she had come more in contact with people who *professed* without possessing than her husband had.

The trouble about Gracie was not so light as she had tried to make it appear to the father. Neither had her attempt to reason the obstinate young daughter into something like graceful yielding been so free from self-pain as she would have him think. It was all about Prof. Ellis, a man who, as Marion expressed it to her husband, was good enough for a teacher, but not at all the sort of man for one so young and so impressible as Gracie to ride away with to an evening entertainment.

"He is the only one I have been in the habit of allowing her to ride with," the father had said, aghast, and then had followed, on Marion's part, a startled exclamation to the effect that she would have trusted her sooner with a dozen of "the boys" with whom she had not been allowed to associate.

"They are better than he," she said, earnestly, and then had followed a long, confidential talk, which had ended in the peremptory, and by no means wisely put, negative to Gracie's plans; and then had followed, on her part, questionings and surmises until at last she understood that this new mother, who had been but a little while ago a stranger to them both, had come between her father and herself, and then had followed, as anyone of sense might have known there would, a scene which was by no means complimentary to Gracie or comforting to the new mother. She had tried to be wise.

"Gracie," she had said, in her gentlest tone, "you know I am a good many years older than you, and I have known Prof. Ellis very well, and I am sure if you realized just the sort of a man he is you would not care to be his familiar friend."

"I don't want to be his familiar friend," Gracie had said, haughtily. "I want to take a ride out to Katie's with him when I have promised to do so." And then her eyes had fallen under the calm of Marion's searching gaze, and her tones had faltered. "At least I do not see that riding out with him is a proof of very great friendship. It is no more than I have done several times with my father's permission."

"But your father was deceived in him, Gracie; he had no means of knowing the sort of man he is, save by his professions, which have been nothing *but* professions for years. Gracie, I know that of him which should make every young girl unwilling to be seen in his society or considered his friend."

Whereupon Gracie's eyes had flashed indignation for a second, then settled into sullenness, while she answered, coldly:

"I should think my father ought to have been capable of judging character a little; he has had something to do with men and life. I do not know why I should not be able to trust myself to *his* judgment."

Marion smiled. It was hard to be patient with this girl. The haughty way in which she retired behind her dignity and said, "*My* father," seemed designed to shut Marion out from ownership in him, and impress her with the sense of the newness of her acquaintance with and entrance into the family.

"Gracie," she said again, after a thoughtful pause, "it may not be known to you that there have been recent developments about Prof. Ellis that make him an undesirable friend for you. I know that, as your teacher, you have learned to look up to and respect him, but he is in some respects unworthy."

There was for a few minutes no response from the sullen-browed girl, with her head bent low over the slate, as if during the intervals of this conversation she had eyes and thought only for the intricate problem before her. Presently she said, in exactly the same tone of repressed indignation which she had used before:

"I repeat that in my judgment *my* father is just as capable of deciding as to what gentlemen are suited to be my friends as a stranger can be."

Marion drew back quickly; she caught her breath hard; this was a trying spot; what should she do or say? What would Ruth Erskine have done in her place? At the same time there was a sense of relief in believing that this young girl's pride only was touched, not her heart. She was simply rebellious that "a stranger," as she chose to call her, should presume to interfere with her friendships.

"I am not a stranger, Gracie," she said, trying to speak in all gentleness. "I am your father's wife, and have at his request assumed responsibilities concerning you, for which I am answerable, not only to him, but to God. When I tell you, therefore, what your father has had no means of knowing, until lately, that Prof. Ellis is the sort of man whom a young lady should shun, you ought to believe me, and to understand that my sole motive is your welfare."

Then was Marion Dennis treated to a brilliant flashing of the handsome eyes of her daughter. The slate and book slid to the floor with an un heeded crash, as Gracie, rising and drawing up her tall form till it equalled her mother's, said, in tones of suppressed passion:

"Marion Wilbur, you have no *right* to speak in that manner of Prof. Ellis, and I will not bear it!"

Then Marion Dennis drew back grieved and frightened, not at her own thrust — that was but the ill-temper of an angry girl — but because she began to fear that this man — this wolf in sheep's clothing, whose chief entertainment hitherto had been to see how well he could play with human hearts — had dared to try his powers on Gracie Dennis. "I hope he will suffer for this," she said, under her breath.

In the meantime what was to be said to the angry girl, whose passion had culminated in this outburst, and who then had thrown herself back into the chair, not weeping, not crushed and bleeding, but excitedly *angry*. And yet, feeling that she had said a very unwise and dangerous thing, and must answer for it — *and yet* not caring just now in what way she might be called upon to answer. Being still in the mood to be glad that she had said it she expected severity, and waited for it.

"Gracie," said Marion, bending toward her, and I do not know that her voice had ever been gentler or her manner more quiet, "you do not mean to hurt *me;* I know you do not. We are too nearly related; we are sisters, *and the Lord Jesus Christ is our Elder Brother*. It is to him that I ask you to listen; it is to his judgment, not mine, that I ask you to defer. Will you lay this matter before him, and wait on your knees for his answer, and abide by it, never minding me? If you will the whole matter will be righted."

Then she turned from her and went down to receive those calls, and get those little thrusts and pin-pricks which pricked so much deeper and left a keener sting because in general they were leveled at her husband instead of herself. Then she went out to that pretty table laid for three, and saw the grave-faced father, and heard his self-reproaches, and held back that which would have made him indignant in the extreme; and held back her own little sigh, and realized that life was not all sweetness, even while Ruth sat at home and envied *her* the brightness of her lot.

CHAPTER XI.

A NEWLY-SHAPED CROSS.

RUTH Erskine, meantime, was keeping up her struggle, having intervals when she seemed to be making headway, and felt as though she had reached higher ground, only to be dropped suddenly down again, into the depths of despair by some unfortunate encounter with the new-comers. No more definite comment on the existing state of things could be made, than is shadowed in that expression, "New-comers." They still continued to be thought of as such in the house. They did not drift into the family ways or customs — they did not assimilate. Everything was so new to them, so unlike their entire former education, that much of the time they stood one side and looked on, instead of mingling and having their individuality lost in the union. So far as Mrs. Erskine was concerned, she did not look on *quietly*. It had been no part of her discipline to learn quietness. She talked everywhere, under the most trying circumstances, and she seemed always to chance upon the things to say that were particularly unfortunate just then and there. This being the case, it is perhaps not strange that the rasping processes were so numerous that there was not time between them for healings. Judge Erskine, on his part, made nearly as little progress. Being a man of faultless grace and bearing, and being noted for fastidiousness, made him preeminently susceptible to wounds in these directions. Generally, he and Ruth maintained the strictest silence toward each other concerning their trials, they having, by tacit consent, agreed upon that as the safest course; but, occasionally, they were rasped into comparing notes. In the hall one morning, where many of their confidential conversations were held, during these days, her father stopped her, with an almost petitioning question:

"Daughter, was it very trying, yesterday, when Mrs. Blakesley called?"

"As trying as it could be, sir," Ruth answered, still smarting so much under that recent infliction that she could not bring her voice to a sympathetic tone. "Mrs. Blakesley, being a woman who hasn't an ounce of brains herself, has, as you may imagine, none to spare for other people. Indeed, father, I sometimes feel as though this matter of making and receiving calls was going to be too complicated a thing for me. I never was fond of such duties, as you may remember, and now it is absolute torture, long drawn out."

"I know it," he said, wincing, and growing paler under each stabbing word from his daughter's lips. "It was all folly, I am afraid. I thought we would try to do just right; but I do not know but we would have felt it less, and they been just as happy, if we had resolutely closed our doors on society altogether, and borne this thing among ourselves."

What these two people needed was some

strong voice to remind them how many, and how much harder troubles life had, than they had been called upon to bear. Despite Marion Dennis' opinion, this is — or it should be — a help. By comparison with other's trials, we ought to be led to feel the lesser nature of our own. Failing in that, it sometimes happens to us to decide as to which of our *own* trials has the heaviest hand.

"I don't think that would have been possible," Ruth answered, her tone somewhat subdued, as it always was, by a realization of her father's deeper wound. "But, I wish with all my heart, I saw a way to escape from some of this calling. There are hundreds, almost, yet to make, and some of them more formidable than any that we have attempted; and the list continues to swell every day."

The father had no answer; he saw no way out. And yet a way was coming, swiftly — one which would help them both out of this dilemma, at least. It was the very next morning that Judge Erskine failed to appear at the breakfast-table and his wife brought word that he was most uncommon restless all night, and pretty fevery, and resisted all her suggestions to give him a good sweat, or to drink any boneset-tea, or even to soak his feet in mustard-water. Consequence was, he didn't feel able to raise his head from his pillow, and wouldn't so much as let her speak of any breakfast, though she *did* tell over several things to him, that she thought he might relish.

Ruth groaned inwardly, not so much at anxiety for her father — his sicknesses were slight affairs soon over, and his most sovereign remedy had hitherto been to be let alone. How, then, had he borne this fearful infliction of sympathy and fertile suggestion?

But the sickness, whatever it was, did not pass away, as others had done. Ruth visiting him, and seeing the fevered face and anxious eyes, felt a nameless dread, and entreated that Dr. Bacon might at once be summoned, being even more alarmed at the fact that her father immediately acquiesced. Dr. Bacon was slow in coming, being a man much sought after in his profession. But he was also unprecedentedly slow in leaving, making a call, the length of which amazed Ruth and at which she did not know whether to be alarmed or relieved. During its continuance Judge Burnham stopped to inquire as to some law papers, and also apparently to make a call, for he tarried after he found that he could not accomplish his original errand, and was in the hall, in the act of leaving, when the doctor came, with slow and thoughtful tread, down-stairs. That gentleman caught at his familiar face, as if it were a relief.

"Ah, good morning, Judge," he said. "This is opportune. May I have a word with you?"

And then he unceremoniously pushed open the library door, and both gentlemen retired within, leaving Ruth perplexed, and perhaps a little annoyed. The door closed upon them. Dr. Bacon was not long in making known his thoughts:

"Judge, are you an intimate friend of this family?"

"Why," said Judge Burnham, hesitating, and flushing a little over the question, "I hardly know whether I may claim exceeding intimacy; the Judge is not apt to have very intimate friends. Perhaps I come as near it as anybody.

Yes, I think I may say I am considered a friend — by *him*, at least. Why, may I ask?"

"Because they need a friend — one who is not afraid of himself or his feelings, and can help them plan, and perhaps execute."

"What on earth do you mean? Is the Judge so very sick?"

"Well, as to that, he is likely to be sick enough — sicker, indeed, than I care to have his daughter realize, just at present. But the *nature* of the sickness is the trouble, It is a very marked case of a very undesirable type of small-pox! Now, don't back out of the nearest door, and leave me in the lurch, for I depend on you."

This last, as Judge Burnham uttered an exclamation of dismay, and stepped backward. The sentence recalled his self-possession.

"Don't be disturbed," he said, and his tones were somewhat haughty. "I have not the slightest intention of fleeing. I shall be glad to serve him and his — his family, to the best of my ability. But what is there for me to do? Is he aware of the situation?"

"Most decidedly so. I didn't mince matters

with him; he is not one that will bear it; he knows all that I do, and is as clear-headed as usual; he knows certain things that must *not* be done. For instance, his daughter Ruth is, on no account, to be allowed to put her head inside the door. He was peremptory about that and must be obeyed, though there is no earthly fear of infection for some days yet; but I have given my word of honor that it shall be as he says. The trouble is, they will be left in the lurch. There isn't a small-pox nurse in the city that I know of. I would have given fifty dollars an hour, almost, for a good one last night, and, besides, the servants must be informed, and they will leave to a man, or a woman. In books you are always reading of heroic servants who are willing to take their lives in their hands and stand by their mistresses through anything. I wish I could find a few of them! I would promise them high wages. Well, now, what you can do first, is to explain the state of affairs to Miss Erskine. I would sooner try to explain to an iceberg, or a volcano — I am never quite sure which she is. And then, if you have any wits, set them to work to establish communication between this house and the outer world. In other words, do what you can for them, *if* you can. You know better than I do whether you are on sufficient terms of intimacy to do anything with her. The old lady must be told, I suppose, though Judge Erskine didn't mention her at all. Perhaps she will want to get out of the house, somewhere, and very likely you can manage that. At least the first thing of importance is to tell Miss Ruth. Will you do it?"

"Y-e-s," said Judge Burnham, speaking slowly and hesitatingly. It was by no means the sort of communication that he desired to make to her, yet he felt an instant desire to stand by her, and, if disagreeable tidings must be given, bear them himself, in whatever alleviating way he might.

"Very well," answered the doctor, promptly. He was spending a great deal of time, on this case, and was getting in haste. "I ought to have been off fifteen minutes ago, but Judge Erskine wanted all the affairs of the nation arranged before I left. He knows what he wants, and, so far as it is within the compass of human possibility, he intends to have it. Will you see Miss Ruth at once, and do what planning you can? Meantime, I will make one more dash for a nurse. No one is to go up to Judge Erskine until I see him again. I fancy he wants to do some thinking for himself. That is his peremptory order, and it will be well enough to obey it. There is no sort of danger of infection now, you understand, but he is quite as well off alone, for a little. Now, I positively must go. I will look in on my way down the square, and report further."

And then the great doctor took himself off leaving Judge Burnham with the worst case on his hands that had ever fallen to his professional life. He walked slowly toward the door, but before he could pass out it was pushed open by Ruth, her face white and frightened. "Judge Burnham what has happened? what is the matter? is my father so very sick? and why am I not to be allowed to go to him?"

"One thing at a time, dear friend," he said, and his voice had a touch of sympathy that could not have escaped her. "Your father is not alarmingly sick, but the sickness is of such a nature that he will not have you exposed to it even for a moment. It was his first thought." And then he pushed a chair forward and gently placed her in it, and sat down beside her, telling her briefly, rapidly, in a half professional manner, all he knew himself. He was a good student of human nature; his success in his profession would have proved that, and he knew it was the surest way to hold her self-controlled and ready for intelligent thought. He had not misjudged her character. She neither cried out nor fainted; she had been pale enough before, but her face whitened a little and she covered her eyes with her hands for an instant. It was a curious revelation to her of the strangeness of these human hearts of ours, when she remembered afterward that, flashing along with the other crowding thoughts as to what, and how, there came the swift memory of the yesterday's talk, and the instant realization of the fact that they would have neither to make nor receive any more of those dreadful calls, for some time, at least. Just a moment of hiding behind those hands and then she was ready for action. "Judge Burnham, have you thought what ought to be done first, and if you have, will you help me?

It makes it harder because my father will not let me come to him. If we could talk together, if he would let me be his nurse, I could—" and then she hesitated, and her lip began to quiver. She remembered that her father was the one person whom she had to love.

"There is no use in talking about that," Judge Burnham said, hastily; "the doctor said he ought, by all means, to be humored in this matter; that it would help to keep him calm, and thus hold the disease in check; you should not have a thought of going to him. Some nurse can surely be found; people will do anything for money. I suppose, Miss Erskine, it will be necessary to tell the other members of the family?"

"Of course," Ruth said, and she tried not to shiver, visibly, as she thought of what Mrs. Erskine might say, and wondered whether she was one of those women who were ignorantly and wildly afraid of infection, and whether there would be a scene with her, and what Susan would do, or say. Then she thought of the servants. "Hannah and Thomas and the rest ought to be told, ought they not, Judge

Burnham?" Then she suddenly roused from her half-suppressed, appealing tones, and rising, said, "How foolishly I am talking! This thing has startled me so. Of course they must be told; and it should be done at once; I will take no unfair advantage of them in any way. Yes, I will tell Mrs. Erskine and my sister. Thank you, Judge Burnham."

And that gentleman began to consider himself as almost dismissed from her presence.

"What can I do for you, first?" he asked her, eagerly; "I am not one of those who are afraid of anything, Miss Erskine; in mortal guise, at least. I am going up to see your father, and since you can not go yourself, you might make me your messenger, to say anything that you would say, that you are willing to have me repeat."

Her eyes brightened. "Thank you," she said, "it is very pleasant to feel that you do not want to desert us. But I will not trouble papa, until I can tell him that we are arranged somehow, and that he need not worry."

She went down first to the kitchen regions and summoned the working force, telling them in brief, clear language, what had fallen upon the house, and offering them each two weeks' wages in advance and good characters. She was young and had not been put to many such tests. They were not "servants in a book," it appeared, for they every one, eagerly caught at their liberty and were nervously anxious to get out of the plague-stricken house, not even desiring to wait until Ruth could get her pocket-book and make good her word. *They* were young and ignorant, and in the great outside world they had friends; life was dear to them. Who shall blame them? And yet, I desire to say, just here, that it is *not* in books only that noble, self-sacrificing exceptions to this form of selfishness are found; I have known kitchens that ought to have glowed with the beauty of the strong, unselfish hearts beating there, through danger, and trial, and harassing toil. It only happened that Ruth Erskine had none of those about her, and, within half an hour after the first word had reached them, she stood alone in her deserted kitchen, trying to get her nerves quiet for the next, and, to her, more trying ordeal. What would those new elements in the house hold say? Was Mrs. Erskine given to hysteria, and would these startling developments produce an attack? Would they want to get away from the house? Could they be gotten away, quietly, to some safe place? Would Susan be willing to go? How would *she* take the news? Ruth puzzled her brain some weary minutes in trying to decide just how they would act, and whether she had courage to tell them, and whether it were not altogether possible that Mrs. Erskine might be moved to make such an outcry as should disturb the sick man, up-stairs. At last she gave over the attempt to arrange their actions for them, and went to summon them to the library, with an air of forced calmness and a determination to have this worst feature of the side issues over, as soon as possible.

CHAPTER XII.

THE CROSS OF HELPLESSNESS

"MY land alive!"

That was what Mrs. Erskine said, when Ruth told her the news. You may have observed that those three words constituted a favorite expression of hers — one which she was apt to use on all occasions, greatly to her stepdaughter's discomfiture. She winced under it now, it seemed so ridiculously inappropriate to the disaster that had come into their midst. While she was trying to impress the situation on the mother and Susan, Dr. Bacon returned. He came directly into the library, as one who had laid aside all the ceremonies of private life, and adopted the business style. He hurried into the midst of the difficulties, being one who, while capable of feeling the most intense and practical sympathy for others, had never learned the art of expressing it other than by actions.

"Miss Ruth, I am afraid it is going to be almost impossible to get a proper nurse for your father. There is a good deal of this abominable disease in the city, now, and the nurses are taxed to the utmost. Ordinary nurses, you know, will not come, and would not do, anyway, So we shall have to manage as well as we can, for a little, until I can look around me and get somebody."

Then Mrs. Erskine came to the front.

"What are you talking about — *nurses?* Who wants one of 'em? miserable, half-awake creatures; not but what I've seen some good ones in my day, but I could beat any of 'em, when it come to a real up-and-down case of sickness; and I can nurse my own husband, you'll find, better than the best of 'em. I brought him back from death's door once, and I will try hard to do it again. A *nurse* is the last kind of a creature that I want to help me."

"But, Mrs. Erskine, I ought not to conceal from you that this is going to be a very decided case of small-pox. The chances of infection, to one who nurses him, will be very great."

"I can't help *that*, you know," she said, determinedly; "*I've* got to be with him, of course. Who would, if his wife wasn't? I don't believe I'll take it. I never was one of them kind that always took things. I have the sick-headache, and that's every blessed thing I do have, except a touch of the rheumatism, now and then; but I never did have a bit of headache, nor nothing, when there was any real sickness on my hands. All the time Susan had the fever I sot up nights, or stood up — a good deal of the time she was that sick that I didn't set down; I jest kept on the trot all night, doing one thing and another. But, all the while, I never had an ache nor a pain about me; and, if I do take it, I might as well as the next one. I ain't a mite afraid of it; not that I'd run into it any quicker than you would, but, when it runs into your own house, and gets hold of your own flesh and blood, or your husband — which is the next thing to that — why, then, I'm one of them kind that has to be on hand. There's no use talkin' — *I'm a going to nurse him*, and all the doctor's in the city can't stop me."

"I assure you, Mrs. Erskine, I haven't the least desire to do so. On the contrary, I appreciate your devotion."

The doctor's tone was earnest — his manner respectful. Mrs. Judge Erskine had evidently risen several degrees in his esteem. She was not a piece of putty, to be gotten out of the way in the least troublesome manner; but a live and very energetic factor in this business. A woman who not only was not afraid of small-pox, but could calmly insist on her right to attend a very bad case of it, was deserving of all respect from him; and he did not, in the least, care how many grammatical errors she made in expressing her determination. In less time than it takes me to tell you of it, the question of attendant on the sick man was settled, and Mrs. Erskine installed as nurse by the relieved doctor, to the satisfaction of all but Ruth. She thought, in dismay, of the misery which her father would be called to endure. How was he, sick and nervous — and she knew he could be fearfully nervous, when only a little ill — to bear the strain of that woman's tongue, when, in health, it was more than he could endure? What would he say to the plan? Would he feel that she might have shielded him from it? Yet how could *she* help it? and, indeed, what else could be done? She had been very nervous over his being left alone. It had seemed to her that she must disregard his positive command and go to him; and it had been such a source of relief and comfort when Judge Burnham announced his intention of going, that she felt she could never forget it. Certainly it would not do to leave him without an attendant. Yet she could not be grateful to the wife for proposing it.

"He can never endure it!" she murmured; and she looked her distress so completely that the doctor was moved to soothe her, when he came back from installing Mrs. Erskine, and giving her directions.

"It will do for a few days, my dear girl; or, at least, for a few hours, until we can look about us, and secure professional assistance. There is not the slightest danger of her taking the disease *now*, you know; indeed, you might be with him yourself, only he is so nervous about you that he will not listen to reason. But she will take good care of him. I really think she understands how to do it."

Ruth made no reply; she could not. She wanted to ask what her father said, and whether he was likely to bear up under such an added weight of misery as this last. But, reflecting that it would not do to say anything of the kind, she took refuge in silence. And the work of rearranging this disorganized and disordered household went on.

In an incredibly short space of time, considering all that had to be planned and arranged, the doctor had done his share of it, given explicit and peremptory directions as to what should, and what should *not* be done, and was gone. As for Judge Burnham, he had gone directly from the sick-room to Judge Erskine's office, on a matter of business for the latter. So the two sisters were left alone in the library, to stare at each other, or out into the street, as they chose.

Susan Erskine had been a very silent looker-on at this morning's confusion Ruth could not tell what she thought. Beyond the first exclamation of surprise, she had expressed no dismay. A little touch of some feeling (what was it?) she had shown once, when her mother was planning, and announcing that she did not intend to take the disease, and, if she did, *she* might as well as anyone.

"Oh, mother!" Susan had said, in a low, distressed tone — a tone full of suppressed feeling of some sort — and her mother had turned on her sharply, with a —

"Well, child, what?"

"Nothing," Susan said, as one who had checked her sentence and was holding herself silent. And thereafter she made no sign.

And so at last these two sisters were stranded in that deserted library. Ruth, on her part, gazing blankly out of the window, watching the hurrying passers-by with a curious sense of wonderment as to what they would think could they know what was transpiring inside. Suddenly she turned from the window with an exclamation of dismay — a thought, which until now had dropped into the background, returned to her.

"There isn't a servant in the house!"

"Why, what has become of them?"

"They fled at the very first mention of the trouble. Never was anything accomplished more rapidly. I thought they had hardly time to reach their rooms when they disappeared around the corner."

"Is it possible!" Susan said, after a moment's silent contemplation. She was both surprised and disappointed. There was nothing in her nature that could respond to that method of bearing one another's burdens, and she did not understand human nature well enough to expect developments in others which were foreign to her own.

"What shall we do about dinner?" Ruth asked, after another interval of silence.

"Why, get it," Susan answered, lightly. She could not comprehend what an impossible thing this was in Ruth's estimation.

"But I — why, I know nothing about it," Ruth said, stammering and aghast.

"I do. There is nothing about a dinner that I do not understand, I believe — that is, a reasonable and respectable dinner. In fact, I know how to do several things that are unreasonable.

I'll go right down-stairs and take a view of the situation."

"I will go with you," Ruth said, heroically. "I don't know anything about such matters, but I can at least show you through the house."

Is it your fortune to know, by experience, just what a deserted look a kitchen can take on in a brief space of time, when the regular inhabitants thereof have made a sudden exit? Just let the fire in the range go down, with unswept ashes littering the hearth, and unwashed dishes filling the tables, and a general smell of departed cookery pervading the air, and you need no better picture of dismalness. Especially is this the case if you survey the scene as Ruth did, without being able to conceive how it was possible ever again to bring order out of this confusion.

"Why, dear me!" said Susan, "things look as though they had stirred them up to the best of their abilities before they left. Where is the hearth-brush kept, Ruth?"

"I am sure I don't know," Ruth said, and she looked helpless and bewildered.

"We'l, then, I'll look for it. We must have

a fire the first thing. I wonder where the kindlings are?"

Then she began to open little doors and crannies, in a wise sort of way, Ruth looking on, not knowing that there were such places to search into. Both hearth-brush and kindlings were found, and Susan attacked the range, while Ruth took up a china cup and set it down again, moved a pile of plates to the side of the table and moved them back again, looking utterly dazed and useless.

"I wonder if this damper turns up or down?"

This from Susan, and her sister turned and surveyed the damper with a grave, puzzled air before she spoke.

"It is no sort of use to ask me. I never even examined the range. I know no more about the dampers than the people on the street do."

"Never mind," said Susan, "the smoke does. It puffs out with one arrangement, and goes up the chimney, as it should, with the other."

"I don't know how we are ever to do it," Ruth said.

"What, make the fire? Why, it is made

already! Don't you hear it roar? This is a splendid range; I should think it would be fun to cook with it. Our stove was cracked, and one door-hinge was broken, and besides it wouldn't bake on the bottom. The *stove* wouldn't, you know — not the broken hinge."

Susan rarely — indeed, I might say never — indulged in reminiscence, and therefore Ruth was touched.

"Why did you keep yourselves so poorly provided for?" she asked, a flush rising on her pale cheek. "I have heard your mother say that you were well supplied with money."

"We were. It was one of my mother's whims, if you choose to call it so. She was continually troubled with the feeling that some day she or I, or — more often, I think — *father*, might need all the money she could save; and I never combated the feeling, except when it intrenched too closely on her own needs. She seemed fairly haunted with the thought."

"How absurd!" said Ruth, and her lip curled.

As for Susan, *her* lips opened, and then closed partly, and whatever she would have uttered remains in oblivion. She closed the damper energetically, and said:

"There, that is conquered! Now, what are we to have for dinner?"

"Why, I ordered roast lamb and its accompaniments," Ruth said, recalling her minute directions given to the skillful cook (she knew how to *order* dinners,) "but, of course, that is out of the question."

"Why, not at all, if you would like it. I know exactly how to roast lamb. But, then, who would eat it?"

"Why, Prof. Stevens and his friend are to dine with us. Oh, they must be sent word not to come! How *can* we send? Who is there to go?"

And Ruth, the complications of her situation pressing upon her in these minor details, looked utterly dismayed.

"Why, Judge Burnham will be our errand-boy — he said so. I met him as he came downstairs, and he told me to say that he would call as soon as he had attended to father's commission, and serve us in any way that we desired. We will have him first recall the invitation to our guests, and then we will send him to the butcher's, the baker's, and the candlestick-maker's.' I shouldn't be surprised if he proved a very useful member of society."

Susan was bent on being cheerful. "Things are not so bad but they might have been worse," she had said, almost as soon as she was told of the trouble.

"Mother says he might have been taken sick down town, and if they had known what the disease was they wouldn't have allowed him to come home. Think of that! But about the roast lamb," she said. "Do you think you and I could compass it, or shall we compel the errand-boy to stay and divide the work with us?"

Then these two girls did what was perhaps the wisest thing for them to do, under the circumstances. They laughed — a real *laugh*.

"Why not?" said Susan. "He is not very sick. The doctor said he didn't think he would be, because he would be well taken care of at the very outset; and he will, you may be sure of that. Mother knows how, and her heart is in it. You may trust her, Ruth, in a time of sickness. And we shall manage nicely. This disconsolate kitchen shall take on new features presently. If I were you I would go right upstairs and be ready to give Judge Burnham his orders when he comes. He is real good and kind. I like him. He will help us in every way. And when you come down again I will have things in train for a first-class dinner."

A new anxiety occurred to Ruth.

"Do you know how to prepare food for sick people?" she asked.

"Indeed I do! The most appetizing little dishes that you can imagine. I've always thought I had a special talent in that direction. We will waylay the doctor the very next time he comes, and find out what he will allow, and then I'll cook it; and you must arrange it daintily with silver, and china, and flowers, you know. They will let us have all sorts of nice things up there for a while, and I think that is the real secret of serving an invalid, having everything arranged tastefully and gracefully."

Ruth turned toward her sister with a very tender smile on her face. She realized that there had been an effort to make her feel that she was in a position to do an important service for her father, and the thoughtfulness of the effort touched her

CHAPTER XIII.

LOOKING FOR AN EASY YOKE.

WEARY days now in store for Ruth Erskine — far more weary and dispiriting than she had imagined were possible to endure. It was such a strange experience to stand at the window and watch passers-by, hurrying out of the neighborhood of the plague-spotted house; crossing the street at most inconvenient points, to avoid a nearer contact. It was so strange to have day after day pass, and never hear the sound of the door-bell — never see the face of a caller — never receive an invitation. In short, it was a sudden shutting out of the world in which she had always lived, and a shutting down into one narrow circle, which repeated itself almost exactly every twenty-four hours. She and Susan must needs be companions now, whether they would or not. They must sit down together three times a day, at table, and go through the forms of eating — not so repulsive a proceeding, by the way, as it had seemed to Ruth it must of necessity be, with no one to serve. Susan had reduced the matter to a system, and produced, as if by magic, the most appetizing dishes, served in faultless style; and, when the strangeness of sitting opposite each other, and having no one to look at or talk to but themselves, began to wear away, they found it a not unpleasant break in the day's monotony to talk together while they waited on each other.

Then there was the sick man's food to prepare, and Susan exhausted her skill, and Ruth contributed of her taste, in graceful adornings. Judge Erskine still adhered to his resolution not to allow his daughter to visit him; so all that could be done for his comfort must be second-handed, but this little was a great relief to heart and brain.

Then there was Judge Burnham, a source of continual comfort. He seemed to be the only one, of all the large circle of friends, who failed to shun the stricken house. He was entirely free from fear, and came and went at all hours, and on all possible errands — market-man, post-man, errand-man in general, and unfailing friend. Not a day passed in which he did not make half a dozen calls, and every evening found him an inmate of the quiet parlor, with a new book, or poem, or, perhaps, only a fresh bouquet of sweet-smelling blossoms, for the sisters. Apparently his tokens of friendship and care were bestowed jointly on *the sisters* — he not choosing between them by a hair-breadth.

Still despite all the alleviating circumstances, the way was weary, and the time hung with increased heaviness on their hands — long hours of daylight, in which there seemed to be nothing to settle to, and in which there was as effectually nowhere to go, as if they were held in by bolts and bars.

"If we were, either of us, fond of fancy work, I believe it would be some relief," Ruth said, wearily, one afternoon, as she closed her book, after pronouncing it hopelessly dull. "Flossy Shipley could spend days in making cunning little worsted dogs, with curly tails, and, if there really were nothing else that she felt she ought to do, I believe she could be quite happy in that!"

Susan laughed.

"One of us ought to have developed that talent, perhaps," she said, brightly. "I don't know why you didn't. As for myself, I never had the time, and, if I had, the materials would have been beyond my purse. But I like pretty things. I have really often wished that I knew how to make some. You don't know how to teach me, I suppose?"

"No, indeed; and, if I did, I'm afraid I shouldn't do it. Nothing ever seemed more utterly insipid to me, though, of course, I never planned any such life as we are having now."

"Look here," Susan said, turning suddenly toward her sister, and dropping the paper which she had been reading. "I have a pleasant thought. We are almost tired of all sorts of books; but there is one Book which never wears out. What if this time of absolute and enforced leisure should have been given us in which to get better acquainted with what it says? What if you and I should begin to study the Bible together?"

Ruth looked gloomy.

"I don't know much about the Bible," she said; "and I don't know how to study it. I read a chapter every day, and, of course, I get some help out of it; but I see so much that I don't understand, and — well, to be frank, so much that it seems to me strange should have been put into the book at all, when necessarily a great deal that we would like to know was left out, that it worries and disappoints me."

She half expected to shock Susan, and looked toward her with determined eyes, ready to sustain her position, in case an argument was produced. But Susan only answered, with a quiet —

"I know; I used to feel very much in the same way, until I had a light given me to go by, which shone upon some of the verses that had been so dark before."

There was no lighting up of Ruth's face.

"I know what you mean," she said, gravely

"You mean that the Bible was a new book to you after you were converted. I have heard a great many people say that, but it doesn't help me as much as you might suppose it would. Of course it made a new book for *me*, because the Bible was never anything to me at all, until I was converted. I have passed years without looking into it; indeed, I may say I *never* read it. When I was a school-girl, I used to find extracts from it in my parsing-book, and some of them seemed to me very lofty sentiments, and several of them I committed to memory, because of the beauty of their construction; but that was the extent of my acquaintance with the book. One of the first things I noticed a Christian say, after I was converted, was about the Bible — what a wonderful book it was to him, and how, every time he read a verse, it opened a new idea. I thought it would be that way with me; but it hasn't been. I love the Bible; that is, I love certain things which I find in it; but it doesn't seem to me as I thought it would. I can't say that I love to study it; or, rather, perhaps I might say I don't know how to study it. I can memorize verses, of course, and I do, somewhat, when I find one that pleases me ; but — well, I never told anyone about it, but it has disappointed me a little."

Now she had shocked Susan ; anyway, she felt sure of it. She had lived long enough, even now, with this plain, quiet sister, to have discovered that the Bible was a great fountain of help to her. She would not be able to understand why it was not the same to Ruth. Neither did Ruth understand it; and, though perhaps she did not realize even this, it was an undertone of longing to get at the secret of the difference between them which prompted her words. But Susan only smiled, in a quiet, unsurprised way, and said :

"I understand you perfectly; I have been over the same ground."

"But you are not there, now?"

"Oh, no, I am not."

"And you learned to love the Bible by studying it?"

"Well, that was the means, of course; but my real help was the revelation which God gave me of himself through the Spirit."

No face could look blanker and gloomier than

Ruth's. She was silent for a few minutes, then she commenced again, her voice having taken on a certain dogged resoluteness of tone as one who thought, " I *will* say it."

" I don't know why I am talking in this way to you; it is not natural for me to be communicative to any person; but I may as well tell you that my religion has been a disappointment to me. It is not what I thought it was. I expected to live such a different life from any that I had lived before. I expected to be earnest, and successful, and happy; and it seems to me that no way was ever more beset with difficulties than mine has been. When I really wanted to do right, and tried, I was apparently as powerless as though I didn't care. I expected to be unselfish, and I am just as selfish, so far as I can see, as I ever was. I struggle with the feeling, and pray over it, but it is there just the same. If for one half hour I succeed in overcoming it, I find it present with me the next hour in stronger force than before. It is all a disappointment. I knew the Christian life was a warfare, but someway I expected more to it than there is; I expected peace out of it, and I haven't got it. I have had my seasons of thinking the whole thing a delusion, so far as I was concerned; but I can not believe that, because in some respects I feel a decided change. I believe I belong to Christ; but I do so shrink from the struggles and trials and disappointments of this world! I feel just as though I wanted to shirk them all. Sometimes I think if He *only would* take me to heaven, where I could rest, I would be *so* grateful and happy."

The hardness had gone out of her face now, and the tears were dropping silently on her closed book.

"Poor girl!" said Susan, tenderly. "Poor, tired heart. Don't you think that the Lord Jesus can rest you anywhere except by the way of the grave? That is such a mistake, and I made it for so long that I know all about it. Don't you hear his voice calling to you to come and rest in him this minute?"

"I don't understand you. I *am* resting in him. That is, I feel sure at times. I feel sure now that he has prepared a place in heaven for me, and will take me there as he says. But I am so tired of the road; I want to drop out from it now and be at rest."

"Haven't you found his yoke easy and his burden light, then?"

"No, I haven't. I know it is my own fault; but that doesn't alter the fact or relieve the weariness."

"Then do you believe that he made a mistake when he said the yoke was easy?"

Ruth arrested her tears to look up in wonder.

"Of course not," she said, quickly. "I know it is owing to myself, but I don't know how to remedy it. There are those who find the statement meets their experience, I don't doubt, but it seems not to be for me."

"But, if that is so, don't you think he ought to have said, 'Some of you will find the burden light, but others of you will have to struggle and flounder in the dark?' You know he hasn't qualified it at all. He said, 'Come unto me and I will give you rest; take my yoke upon you, for it is light.' And he said it to all who are 'heavy laden.'"

"Well," said Ruth, after a thoughtful pause, "I suppose that means his promise to save the soul eternally. I believe he has done that for me."

"But is that all he is able or willing to do? If he can save the soul eternally can not he give it peace and rest here?"

"Why, of course he could, if it were his will; but I don't know that he has ever promised to do so."

"Don't you? Do you suppose he who hates sin has made us so that we can not keep from constantly grieving him by falling into sin, and has promised us no help from the burden until we get to heaven? I don't think that would be entire salvation."

"What *do* you mean?" Ruth asked, turning a full, wondering gaze on her sister. "You surely don't believe that people are perfect in this world?"

"Pass that thought, just now, will you? Let me illustrate what I mean. I found my besetting sin to be to yield to constant fits of ill-temper. It took almost nothing to rouse me, and the more I struggled and tossed about in my effort to *grow* better the worse it seemed to me I became. If I was to depend on progress sive goodness, as I supposed, when was I to begin to grow *toward* a better state; and when I succeeded should I not really have accomplished my own rescue from sin? It troubled and tormented me, and I did not gain until I discovered that there were certain promises which, with conditions, meant me. For instance, there was one person who, when I came in contact with her, invariably made me angry. For months I never held a conversation with her that I did not say words which seemed to me afterward to be very sinful, and which angered her. This after I had prayed and struggled for self-control. One day I came across the promise, 'My grace is sufficient for thee.' Sufficient for what? I asked, and I stopped before the words as if they had just been revealed. I found it to be unlimited as to quantity or time. It did not say, 'After you have done the best you can — struggled for years and gained a little — then my grace shall be sufficient.' It did not say, 'My grace is sufficient for the great and trying experiences of this life, but not for the little every-day annoyances and trials which tempt you — you must look out for yourself.'

It was just an unlimited promise — 'My grace is sufficient — not for my saints, for those who have been faithful and successful, but for *thee*.' Having made that discovery, and felt my need, I assure you I was not long in claiming my rights. Now, I want to ask you what that promise means?"

"'My grace is sufficient for thee,'" Ruth repeated, slowly, thoughtfully. Then she paused, while Susan waited for the answer, which came presently, low-toned and wondering.

"I'm sure I don't know. I read the verse only yesterday, but it didn't occur to me that it had any reference to *me*. I don't know what I thought about it."

"But what does it seem to you that it says? Christ meant something by it, of course. What was it?"

"I don't know," she said again, thoughtfully. "That is, why it *can't* mean what it appears to, for then there would be nothing left to struggle about."

"Well, has Christ ever told you to struggle? On the contrary, hasn't he told you to rest?"

"It seems to me," said Ruth, after revolving

that thought, or some other, in silence for several minutes — "it seems to me that one who thought as you do about these things would be claiming perfection; and if there is one doctrine above another that I despise it is just that. I know one woman who is always talking about it, and claiming that she hasn't sinned in so many months, and all that nonsense; and really she is the most disagreeable woman I ever met in my life."

"Look here," said Susan. "Do you rely on the Lord Jesus for salvation? That is, do you believe you are a sinner, and could do nothing for yourself, and he just had to come and do it for you, and present your claim to Heaven through himself?"

"Why, of course there is no other way. I *know* that I am a sinner; and I know it is wonderful in him to have been willing to save me; but he has."

"Well, now, aren't you afraid to claim that, for fear people will think that you saved yourself?"

"I don't understand," Ruth said, gravely.

"Don't you? Why, you fear to claim Christ's

promise to you — that his grace is *now* sufficient for every demand that you choose to make on it — for fear people will think you consider yourself perfect. Why should they not, just as readily, think that because you relied on Christ for final salvation therefore you relied on yourself?"

"That is a foolish contradiction."

"Yes; isn't the other?"

"I never heard anybody talk as you do," was Ruth's answer.

"I haven't a different Bible from yours," Susan said, smiling. "You admit to me that the promise about which we are talking is in yours, and you read it yesterday. What I wonder is, what you think it **means**."

CHAPTER XIV.

"THROUGH A GLASS, DARKLY."

THE last was but the beginning of many talks which those two sisters held together concerning the meaning of the promises which Christ had made to his children. During the time Ruth received and accepted some new ideas; but it must be admitted that it was her intellect which accepted them, rather than her heart. She acknowledged that the Lord had plainly said his grace was sufficient for them, and that, having been tempted, he was able to succor those who were tempted; and that there should no temptation take his children except such as they were able to bear, because the faithful God would provide a way of escape. All these, I say, she admitted; they were plainly written in his word and *must* mean what they said. Still she went on, being tempted and yielding to the temptation, struggling against the gloom and unrest of her lot—struggling fiercely against the providence which had come between her and the Father, whom she began to realize she had worshiped rather than loved— struggling, fighting, baffled, wounded, defeated —only to rise up and struggle afresh, all the while admitting with her clear brain-power that he said: "As thy day, so shall thy strength be." Why did she not have the strength? She dimly questioned with herself, occasionally, the why; she even deemed herself ill-treated because none of the promised strength came to her; but she passed over the searching question of the Lord to his waiting suppliant: "*Believe* ye that I am able to do this?" Had the Lord Jesus Christ appeared to Ruth in bodily presence and asked her this question she realized afterward that she would have been obliged to answer: "Oh, no, I don't. You say you are able, and you say you are willing, and I believe that the words are yours, and that you have all power in heaven and earth, and yet — and yet — I *don't* believe that you will do it for me." To such strange and unaccountable depths of absurdity does unbelief lead us!

At last there came a day when Susan and she could not talk calmly about these things or any other — could not talk at all — could only weep, and wait, and kneel and dumbly pray, and then wait again, while life and death struggled fiercely together for the victim up-stairs, and it seemed that death would be the victor. Many days passed, and the dead-weight of enforced endurance still held Ruth a prisoner, and still she rebelled against the providence that had hemmed her in and shut her away from her father; still she rebelled at the thought of the nurse who bent over him in tireless watch, long before all attempts at securing outside help had been abandoned, Dr. Bacon having expressed himself more than satisfied.

"Never a better nurse took hold of a case," he said, emphatically, to Ruth. "If your father recovers, and I can not help feeling hopeful, he will owe it more to her care than to any other human effort. She seems to know by instinct what and when and how, and I believe the woman never sleeps at all. She is just as alert and active and determined to-day as she was the first hour she went into his room, and the vigil has been long and sharp. I tell you what, Miss Ruth, you begin to understand, don't you, what this woman was raised up for? She was planned for just such a time as this. No money would have bought such nursing, and it has been a case in which nursing was two-thirds of it. She ought to be a *professional* nurse this minute. Shall I find a place for her when her services are not needed here in that capacity any longer? She could command grand wages."

The well-meaning doctor had essayed to bring a smile to Ruth's wan face; but it was made evident to him that he understood disease better than he did human nature — at least the sort of human nature of which she was composed. She drew herself up proudly, and her tone was unusually and unnecessarily haughty as she said:

"You forget, Dr. Bacon, that you are speaking of *Mrs. Erskine*."

Then the doctor shrugged his shoulders, and,

with a half-muttered "I beg pardon," turned away.

"More of an iceberg than ever," he muttered, a little louder, as he went down the hall. "I don't know what Burnham is about, I am sure. I hope it is the other one he means."

And then he slammed the door a little. He had left Ruth in a rage with him and with events and with her own heart. She resented his familiarity with the name which that woman bore, and she resented the fact that she bore the name. She was bitterly jealous of Mrs. Erskine's position by that sick-bed. She did not believe in her nursing abilities. She knew she was fussy and officious and ignorant, three things that were horrible in a nurse. She knew her father must be a daily sufferer because of this. She by no means saw "what that woman was raised up for," or why she should have been permitted to come in contact with *her*. Every day she chafed more under it, and the process made her grow hard and cold and silent to the woman's daughter. So by degrees the burden grew heavier, and Susan, feeling that no word of hers could help, maintained at last a tender, patient silence, that to Ruth's sore, angered heart was in itself almost an added sting.

It was in this spirit that they drew near to the hour when the question of life and death would be determined. Ruth's heart seemed like to burst with the conflict raging in it — sorrow, anxiety, despair — she knew not what to call the burden, but she knew it was a *burden*. She spent hours in her own room, resenting all interruptions, resenting every call from Susan to come down and take a little nourishment; even almost disposed to resent the bulletins for which she waited breathlessly as they were from time to time spoken through the keyhole in Susan's low-toned voice. " He is no worse than he was half an hour ago, Ruth;" or, "The doctor thinks there must be a change before night;" or, " Dear Ruth, he murmured your name a little while ago' the doctor said."

Presently Ruth came out of her room and down to the library — came toward Susan sitting in the little rocker with her Bible in her lap, and said, speaking in a low tone so full of pent-up energy that in itself it was startling:

" Susan, if you know how to pray at all, kneel

down now and pray for *him*—I can't. I have been trying for hours, and have forgotten how to pray."

Without a word of reply Susan arose quickly and dropped on her knees, Ruth kneeling beside her, and then the words of prayer which filled that room indicated that one heart, at least, knew how to pray, and felt the presence of the Comforter pervading her soul. Long they knelt there, unwilling, it seemed, to rise, even after the audible prayer ceased. And it was thus that Judge Burnham found them, as with light, quick steps he crossed the hall in search of them, saying, as he entered:

"Courage, dear friends, the doctor believes that there is strong reason now for hope."

The crisis passed, Judge Erskine rallied rapidly, much more rapidly than those who had watched over him in the violence of his sickness had deemed possible. And it came to pass that, after a few more tedious days of waiting, his room was opened once more to the presence of his daughter. Fully as she had supposed that she realized his illness, she was unprepared for the change which it had wrought, and could hardly suppress a cry of dismay as she bent over him. Long afterward she wondered at herself as she recalled the fact that her first startled rebellious thought had been that there was not such a striking contrast now between him and his wife.

There was another disappointment in store for her. She had looked forward to the time when she might reign in that sick-room — might become her father's sole nurse in his convalescence, and succeed in banishing from his presence that which must have become so unendurable. She discovered that it was a difficult thing to banish a wife from her husband's sick-room. Mrs. Erskine was, apparently, serenely unconscious that her presence was undesired by Ruth. She came and went freely; was cheery and loquacious, as usual; discoursed on the dangers through which Judge Erskine had passed, and reiterated the fact that it was a mercy she didn't take the disease, until, actually, Ruth was unable to feel that even this was a mercy! There was a bitterer side to it. Her father had changed in more ways than one. It appeared that his daughter's unavailing grief for him, in becoming the victim of such a nurse, was all wasted pity

He had not felt it an infliction. His voice had taken a gentle tone, in which there was almost tenderness, when he spoke to her. His eyes followed her movements with an unmistakable air of restfulness. He smiled on his daughter; but he asked his wife to raise his head and arrange his pillow. How was this to be accounted for? How could a few short weeks so change his feelings and tastes?

"She *is* a born nurse," Ruth admitted, looking on, and watching the cheery skill with which she made all things comfortable. "Who would have supposed that she could be other than fussy? Well, all persons have their mission. If she could have filled the place of a good, cheerful, hospital nurse, how I should have liked her, and how grateful I should feel to her now!" And then she shuddered over the feeling that she did not now feel toward her an atom of gratitude! She looked forward to a moment when she could be left alone with her father. Of course he was grateful to this woman. His nature was higher than hers. Beside, he knew what she had done, and borne for him, here in this sick-room. Of course he felt it, and was so thoroughly a gentleman that he would show her, by look and action, that he appreciated it; but, could his daughter once have him to herself for a little while, what a relief and comfort it would doubtless be to him. Even over this thought she chafed. If this woman *only* held the position in the house which would make it proper for her to say, "You may leave us alone now, for awhile. My father and I wish to talk; I will ring when you are needed" — with what gracious and grateful smiles she could have said those words! As it was, she planned.

"Don't you think it would be well for you to go to another room, and try to get some rest?"

"Yes," said Judge Erskine, turning his head, and looking earnestly at her; "if any human being ever needed rest, away from this scene of confusion, I think you must."

"Bless your heart, child" (with a good-natured little laugh)! "I've rested ever so much. When you get used to it, you can sleep standing up, with a bowl of gruel in one hand, and a bottle of hot water in the other, ready for action. Just as soon as the anxiety was off, I got rest; and, while I was anxious, you know, I lived on that — does about as well as sleep for keeping up strength; I guess you tried it yourself, by the looks of your white cheeks and great big eyes! Land alive! I never see them look so big; did you, Judge? But Susan says you behaved like a soldier. Well, I knew you would. I says, to myself, says I, 'She is made of the stuff that will bear it, and do her best;' and it give me strength to do my best for your pa, 'cause I knew you was depending on me. Says I, 'I've got two sides to this responsibility now; there's the Judge, lying helpless, and knowing that every single thing that's done for him, for the next month or so, must come through me; and there's his daughter downstairs, trusting to me to bring him through;' and I did my level best."

And then Ruth shuddered. It was impossible for her to feel anything but repulsion.

At last Susan — wise-hearted Susan — came to her rescue. She had imperative need for "mother" in the kitchen, for a few minutes. Ruth watched eagerly, as she waddled away, until the door closed after her, then turned with hungry eyes toward her father, ready to pour out her pent-up soul, as she never had done before. His eyes were turned toward the door, and he said, as the retreating footsteps were lost to them :

"If you have joy in your heart, daughter — as I know you have — for the restoration of your father, you owe it, under God, to that woman. I never even imagined anything like the utter self-abnegation that she showed. Disease, in its most repulsive, most loathsome form, held me in its grasp, until I know well I looked less like a human being than I did like some hideous wild animal. Why, I have seen even the doctor start back, overcome, for a moment, by the sight! But she never started back, nor faltered, in her patient, persistent, tender care, through it all. We both owe her our gratitude and our love, my daughter."

Do you know Ruth well enough to understand that she poured out no pent-up tide of tenderness upon her father, after that? She retired into her old silent self, to such a degree that the father looked at her wonderingly, at first, then half wearily, and turned his head and closed his eyes, that he might rest, since she had nothing to say to him.

It was two or three days afterward that she tried again. In the meantime, she had chided herself sharply for her folly. Why had she allowed herself to be so cold — so apparently heartless — when her heart was so full of love? Was she really so demoralized, she asked herself, that she would have her father other than grateful for the care which had been bestowed? Of *course* he was grateful, and of course he desired to show it, as any noble nature should. After all, what had he said but that they both owed her a debt of gratitude and love?

"So we do," said Ruth, sturdily. "I should love a dog who had been kind to him." And then she suppressed an almost groan over the startling thought that, if this woman had been *only a dog*, she could have loved!

But she was left alone with her father again. He had advanced to the sitting-up stage, and she was to sit with him and amuse him, while Mrs. Erskine attended to some outside matter, Ruth neither knew nor cared what, so that she went away. She was tender and thoughtful, shading her father's weakened eyes from the light, picking up his dropped handkerchief, doing a dozen little nothings for him, and occasionally speaking some tender word. He was not disposed to talk much beyond asking a few general questions as to what had transpired during his absence from the world. Then, presently, he broke an interval of silence, during which he had sat with closed eyes, by asking:

"Where is Susan?"

"Susan!" his daughter repeated, half startled. "Why, she is in the kitchen, I presume; she generally is, at this hour of the morning. She has had to be housekeeper and cook and I hardly know what not, during these queer days. She has filled all the posts splendidly! I don't know what you would have eaten but for her."

Here Ruth paused a moment, to be gratified over her own advance in goodness. At least she could speak freely, and in praise of Susan. Then she said:

"Do you want anything, father, that Susan can get for you?"

He unclosed his eyes, and looked at her with a full, meaning smile, as he said, slowly:

"I was not thinking of *that* Susan, my dear; I meant my wife. You may call her, if you will; I feel somewhat tired, and she knows just how to fix me for rest."

Imagine Ruth Erskine going down the hall, down the stairs, through the library, out through the back hall, away to the linen-closet, and saying, to Mrs. Judge Erskine, in a low tone:

"Father wants you, ma'am!"

"Bless his heart!" said Mrs. Erskine, dropping the pile of fresh linen she was fumbling in. "I hope he hasn't been fretty 'cause I staid so long!"

Then she fled up the stairs.

Well, you are not very well versed in the knowledge of the depths of the human heart, if you need to be told that this last experience was the bitterest drop in Ruth's cup of trouble. Hitherto it had been her father and herself, bearing together a common trial. Now she felt that, someway, she had lost her father, and gained nothing — rather, *lost* — that she had sunken in her own estimation, and that she was alone!

CHAPTER XV.

RESTS.

IT took some time for the Erskines to find their way back into the world — rather it took the world many weeks to be willing to receive them. What was reasonable caution at first became not only annoying but ludicrous, as the weeks went by, and common-sense suggested that all possibility of danger from contact with them was past; there were those who *could not* believe that it would eve⋯ ⋯fe to call on them again. Ruth, on her ⋯ ⋯t worry over this, but suggested ⋯ ⋯at it would be an almost infinit⋯ ⋯wo-thirds of their calling acq⋯ ⋯ould continue frightened for the rest of their lives.

In the domestic world it made more trouble. Servants — an army of them — who were marshaled to and from intelligence offices, looked askance at the doors and windows, as if they half expected the demon of small-pox to take visible shape and pounce upon them, and it was found to be only the worst and most hopeless characters who had ventured into doubtful quarters, so that for days Susan was engaged in well-managed skirmishes between girls who professed everything and knew nothing.

Ruth had long before retired, vanquished from this portion of the field, and agreed that her forte did not lie in that direction. "I haven't the least idea where it lies," she said aloud, and gloomily. But she was in her own room, and the door was locked, and there was no other listener than the window-light, against which her brown head wearily leaned. She had not yet reached the point where she was willing to confess her disappointment at life to anybody else, but in truth it seemed that the world was too small for her. She was not needed at home, nor elsewhere, so far as she could see. Her father, as he relapsed into old duties, did not seek his former confidential footing with her; indeed, he seemed rather to avoid it, as one who might fear lest his own peace would be shaken. So Ruth thought at first, but one little private talk with him had dispelled the probability of that.

"I want to tell you something, daughter," he had said to her when they were left alone in the library, the first day of his return to office-life. "At least I owe it to you to tell you something. I waited until I had really gotten back into the work-a-day world again, because of a half recognized fear which I see now was cowardly and faithless, that old scenes would recall old feelings. I had an experience, my daughter, during those first few days when the Lord shut me out from you all. My Christian faith did not sustain me as it ought to have done. I mean by that, that it was not the sort of faith which it ought to have been. I rebelled at the fierceness of the fire in which I had been placed. I felt that I could not bear it; that it was cruel and bitter. Most of all, I rebelled at the presence of my wife. I felt that it was too much to be shut away from everything that life holds dear, and to be shut up with that which had hitherto made life miserable. I can not tell you of the struggle, of the hopeless beatings of my bruised head against the bars of its cage. It almost unmans me even to think of those hours." And Judge Erskine paused and wiped the perspiration from his forehead. "I will just hurry over the details," he said at last. "There came an hour when I began to dimly comprehend that my Redeemer was only answering some of the agonizing prayers that I had of late been constantly putting up to him. I had prayed, Ruth, for strength to do my whole duty, and in order to do it I plainly saw that I must feel differently from what I had been feeling; that I must get over this shrinking from a relation which I deliberately brought upon myself, and one which I was bound, by solemn covenant, to sustain. I must have help; I must submit, not only, but I must learn to be pitiful toward, and patient with, and yet how *could* I? Christ showed me how. He let me see such a revelation of my own selfishness, and hardness, and pride, as made me abhor myself in 'dust and ashes,' and then he let me see such a revelation of human patience, and tenderness, and self-abnegation, as filled me with gratitude and respect. Ruth, he has given me much more than I asked. I prayed for patience and tenderness and he gave me not only those, but such a feeling of respect for one who could so entirely forget herself, and do for another what my wife did for me, that I feel able to cherish her all the rest of my life. In short, daughter, I feel that I could take even the vows of the marriage-covenant upon my lips now, and mean them in all simplicity and singleness of heart. And having taken them long ago I ratify them now, and mean to live by them as long as life lasts to us both, so help me God. In all this I do not forget the sin, nor the suffering which that sin has entailed upon you, my dear, precious daughter, but I feel that I must do what I can to atone for it, and that shirking my duty, as I have been doing in the past, does not help you to bear your part. I know you have forgiven me, Ruth, and I know that God has. He has done more than that. In his infinite love and compassion he has made the cross a comfort. And now, daughter, I never wish to speak of this matter again. You asked me, once, if I wished you to call her mother. I have no desire to force your lips to what they do not mean, nor to oblige you to bear any more cross for your father, than the sin has, in itself, laid upon you, but if, at any time in your future life, you feel that you care to say, "Mother," it will be a pleasant sound to my ears."

Ruth reflected, afterward, with a sense of thankfulness, that she had grace enough left to bend forward and kiss her father's white forehead, and pass her hand tenderly over the moist locks of gray hair above his temples. Then she went out and went away. She could have spoken no word just then. She was struggling with two conflicting feelings. In her soul she was glad for her father; that he had got help, and that his heavy cross was growing into peace. But all the same — she felt now, and felt with a dull aching at her heart which refused to be comforted, that she herself had not found peace in it; that it was, if anything, more bitter than ever, and that she had lost her father. Is it any wonder that life to her stretched out gloomily?

Many changes had taken place during their

enforced exile from the world. Eurie Mitchell had married and gone, and Flossy Shipley had married and gone, both of them to new homes and new friends, and both of them had, by their departure, made great gulfs in Ruth's life. They had written her characteristic notes along with their wedding cards. Eurie's ran thus:

"*Dear Ruth*—I fancy you bearing it like a martyr, as I know you can. I always said you would make a magnificent martyr, but I am so sorry that the experiment has come in such a shape that we can't look on and watch its becomingness. Also, I am very sorry that you can not be present to see me 'stand up in the great big church without any bonnet!' which is the way in which our baby characterizes the ceremony. In fact, I am almost as sorry about that as I am that father should have been out of town during the first few days of Judge Erskine's illness, and so given that Dr. Bacon a chance to be installed. Father doesn't happen to agree with him on some points, and the care of small-pox patients is one thing in which they totally differ. However, your father is going on finely, so far, I hear, and you know, my dear, that Dr. Bacon *is very* celebrated; so be as brave as you can and it will all come out right, I dare say. In fact we *know* it will. Isn't that a comfort? There are ever so many things that I might say if I could, but you know I was never able to put my heart on paper. So imagine some of the heart-thoughts which beat for you, while I sign myself for the last time,

"Eurie Mitchell."

Ruth laughed over this note. ,' It is so exactly like her," she murmured. "I wonder if she will ever tone down?"

Flossy's was smaller, daintier, delicately perfumed with the faintest touch of violets, and read:

"*Dear, Precious Friend* — 'The eternal God is thy refuge, and underneath are the everlasting arms.' How safe you are! 'Oh, thou afflicted, tossed with tempest and not comforted! Behold, I will lay thy stones with fair colors; with everlasting kindness will I have mercy on thee, saith the Lord, thy Redeemer.' Blessed Jesus, do for Ruth 'As thou hast said.' This is Flossy Shipley's prayer for her dear friend, whom she will love and cherish forever."

Over this note Ruth shed hot tears. She was touched and comforted and saddened ; she realized more than ever before what a spiritual loss Flossy's going was to be to her, and she did not come closer to the One who would have made amends for all losses.

Perhaps she had never felt the dreariness of her existence more than she did on a certain evening, some weeks after the household had settled into its accustomed routine of life, which was like and yet utterly unlike what that life had been before the invasion of disease.

It was dark outside, and the rain was falling heavily; there was little chance of relief from monotony by the arrival of guests. Ruth wandered aimlessly through the library in search of a book that she felt willing to read, and, finding none, turned at last to the sitting-room, where Judge Erskine and his wife were sitting. Secure in the prospect of rain, and therefore seclusion, he had arrayed himself in dressing-gown and slippers, and was resting his scarred, seamed face among the cushions of the easy-chair, enjoying a luxury, which was none other than that of having his gray hair carefully and steadily brushed, the brush passing with the regularity of a sentinel on its slow, soothing track, guided by his wife's hand, while Judge Erskine's face bore unmistakable signs of reposeful rest. There was that in the scene which irritated Ruth almost beyond control. She passed quickly through the room, into the most remote corner of the alcove, which was curtained off from the main room, and afforded a retreat for the piano, and a pretext for any one who desired to use it and be alone. It was not that *she* had ever waited thus upon her father; she had never thought of approaching him in this familiar way. Even had she dared to do so, their make-up was, after all, so utterly dissimilar that, what was evidently a sedative to him, would have driven his daughter fairly wild. To have any one, however dear and familiar, touch her hair, draw a brush through it, would have irritated her nerves in her best days. She thought of it then, as she sat down in the first seat that she reached, after the friendly crimson curtains hid her from those two — sat with her chin resting in her two listless hands, and tried to wonder what she should do if she were forced to lie among the cushions of that easy-chair in there, and have *that* woman brush her hair.

"I should choke her, I know I should!" she said, with sudden fierceness; and then, with scarcely less fierceness of tone and manner added: "I hope it will never be my awful fate to have to be taken care of by her, or to have to endure the sight of her presence about any one I love. Oh, what is the matter with me! I grow wicked every hour. What *will* become of me?"

After all, there were those who were not afraid of the rain, and were not to be kept from their purposes by it. Ruth listened indifferently at first, then with a touch of eagerness, to the sound of the bell, and the tones in the hall, and then to the sound of Judge Burnham's step as he was being shown to the sitting-room. The new help had been in the house just long enough to discover that he was a privileged and unceremonious guest.

"Ah!" he said, pausing in the doorway "Am I disturbing? Sick to-night, Judge?"

"Come in," said Judge Erskine's hearty voice. "No, I am not sick, only dreadfully lazy and being petted. When I was a boy, and mother used to brush my hair, nothing soothed and rested me so much, and I find I haven't lost the old habit. Have a chair, and tell us the evening news. I haven't been out of the house since dinner."

"Nothing specially new," said Judge Burnham, dropping into an easy-chair and looking around him inquiringly. "Where are the ladies?"

"Why," said Mrs. Erskine, brushing away steadily, "Susan is in the kitchen; she mostly is these days. Such a time as we are having with servants; I wonder she don't get sick of the whole set and tell them to tramp. Just now, though, she has got hold of one who seems willing enough to learn; and Susan heard her pa say this noon that he believed he would like some muffins once more, so she is down there trying to teach Mollie about setting muffins, and beating of it into her to let them alone in the morning till *she* gets down to 'tend to them."

"Why," said Judge Erskine, in a tone of tenderness that jarred Ruth's ears, "I wonder if she is attending to that? What a child she is! She will wear herself out waiting on me."

"There ain't a selfish streak about her," Mrs. Erskine said, complacently " nor never was. But la! you needn't fret about her, Judge; she loves to do it. She went down in the first place to 'tend to that, but she has got another string to her bow now; she found out that Mollie didn't know how to read writing, and had a letter from her mother that she couldn't make out, so Susan read it to her, and the next thing was to write her an answer, and she is at that now."

"And where is Miss Ruth?" questioned Judge Burnham, the instant this long sentence was concluded.

"Why, she is moping—that's the best name I know for it. She is back there in the alcove. I thought she went to play, but she hasn't played a note. That child needs a change. I'm just that worried about her that her white face haunts me nights when I'm trying to sleep. She has had an awful hard siege; her pa so sick, and she obliged to keep away from him, and not being sure whether I knew more than a turnip about taking care of him — I wonder how she stood it. And I'm just afraid she will break down yet. She needs something to rest her up and give her some color in her cheeks. I keep telling her pa that he ought to do something."

"Suppose I go and help her mope," Judge Burnham said, rising in the midst of a flow of words, and speedily making his way behind the red curtains.

He came over to Ruth, holding out both hands to greet her.

"How do you do?" he said, and there was tender inquiry in the tone. "You didn't know I was in town, did you? I came two days sooner than I had hoped."

"I didn't know you were out of town," said Ruth. "I thought you had deserted us like the rest of our friends."

"So you didn't get my note?" he asked, looking blank. "Well, never mind; it was merely an explanation of an absence which I hoped you might notice. Mrs. Erskine says you are moping, Ruth. Is it true? She says you need a change and something to rest you up. I wish you would let me give you a change. Don't you think you could?"

"A change!" Ruth repeated, with a little laugh, and there was color enough in her cheeks just then.

"Why should *I* need a change? What do you mean?"

"I mean a great deal. I want to give you such a change as will affect all your future life and mine. I would like to have you change name and home. Oh, Ruth, I would like to devote my life to the business of 'resting you up.' Don't you believe I can do it?"

Now, I am sure there is no need for me to give you Ruth Erskine's answer. You probably understand what it was. Unless I am mistaken, you understand her better than she did herself. Up to this very moment she actually had not realized what made up the bulk of her unrest this week. No, not the bulk either; there were graver questions even than this one which might well disturb her, but she had not understood her own footing with Judge Burnham, nor had scarcely a conception of his feelings toward her.

The low murmur of talk went on, after a little, behind the red curtains, and continued long after Judge Erskine and his wife went up-stairs. Just as he was turning out the gas in their dressing-room, that gentleman said:

"Unless I am mistaken, Judge Burnham would like to give Ruth a decided change."

"Land alive!" said Mrs. Erskine, taking in his meaning, after a little, "I declare, now you speak of it, I shouldn't wonder if he did." Then she added, kindly, genuinely: "And I'm sure I hope it's true; I tell you that child needs resting up.

CHAPTER XVI.

SHADOWED JOYS.

ONE of the first experiences connected with Ruth's new life was a surprise and a trial. She did not act in the matter as almost any other young lady would have done. Indeed, perhaps, you do not need to be told that it was not her *nature* to act as most others would in like circumstances. She kept the story an entire secret with her own heart. Not even her father suspected that matters were settled; perhaps, though, this last is to be accounted for by the fact that Judge Burnham went away, again on business, by the early train the morning after he had arranged for Ruth's change of home and

name, and did not return again for a week.
During that week, as I say, Ruth hugged her
new joy and kept her own counsel. Yet it was
joy. Her heart was in this matter. Strangely
enough it had been a surprise to her. She had
understood Judge Burnham much less than
others, looking on, had done, and so gradual and
subtle had been the change in her own feeling
from almost dislike to simple indifference, and
from thence to quickened pulse and added interest in life at his approach, that she had not in
the remotest sense realized the place which he
held in her heart until his own words revealed it
to her. That she liked him better than any
other person, she began to know; but when she
thought about it at all it seemed a most natural
thing that she should. It was not saying a great
deal, she told herself, for she really liked very
few persons, and there had never been one so
exceptionally kind and unselfish and patient.
What should she do but like him? Sure
enough! And yet, when he asked her to be his
wife, it was as complete a surprise as human experiences could ever have for her. Desolate,
afflicted, deserted, as she felt, it is no wonder

that the revelation of another's absorbed interest in her filled her heart.

As I say, then, she lived it alone for one delightful week. It was the afternoon of the day on which she expected Judge Burnham's return, and she knew that his first step would be an interview with her father. She determined to be herself the bearer of the news to Susan. During this last week, whenever she thought of her sister, it had been a tender feeling of gratitude for all the quiet, unobtrusive help and kindness that she had shown since she first came into the family. Ruth determined to show that she reposed confidence in her, and for this purpose sought her room, ostensibly on some trivial errand, then lingered and looked at a book that lay open, face downward, as if to keep the place, on Susan's little table. Susan herself was arranging her hair over at the dressing bureau. Ruth never forgot any of the details of this afternoon scene. She took up the little book and read the title. "The Rest of Faith." It had a pleasant sound *Rest* of any sort sounded pleasantly to Ruth She saw that it was a religious book, and she dimly resolved that some other time, when she felt quieter, had less important plans to carry out, she would read this book, look more closely into this matter, and find, if she could, what it was that made the difference between Susan's experience and her own. That there was a difference was *so* evident; and yet, without realizing it, Ruth's happiness of the last few days was making her satisfied with her present attainments spiritually. No, not exactly satisfied, but willing to put the matter aside for a more convenient season.

"I have something to tell you that I think you will be interested to hear," she said, at last, still turning the leaves of the little book, and feeling more embarrassed than she had supposed it possible for *her* to feel.

"Have you?" said Susan, brightly. "Good! I like to hear new things, especially when they have to do with my friends." And there was that in her tone which made her sister understand that she desired to convey the thought that she felt close to Ruth, and wanted to be held in dear relations. For the first time in her life Ruth was conscious of being willing.

"Judge Burnham is to return to-day."

"Yes, I heard you speaking of it."

There was wonderment in Susan's tone, almost as well as words could have done. It said: "What is there specially interesting in that?"

"Do you feel ready to receive him in a new relation?" Ruth asked, and she was vexed to feel the blood surging into her cheeks. "I think he has a desire to be very brotherly."

"Oh, Ruth!"

There was no mistaking Susan's tone this time. She had turned from the mirror and was surveying her sister with unmistakably mournful eyes, and there was astonished sorrow in her tones. What could be the trouble! Whatever it was Ruth resented it.

"Well," she said haughtily, "I seem to have disturbed as well as surprised you. I was not aware that the news would be disagreeable."

"I beg your pardon, Ruth. I *am* very much surprised. I had not supposed such a thing possible."

"Why, pray?"

"Why, Ruth, dear, he is not a Christian?"

It would be impossible to describe to you the

consternation in Susan's face and voice, and the astonishment in Ruth's.

"Well," she said again, "it is surely not the first time you were conscious of that fact. He will be in no more danger in that respect with me for a wife. At least I trust he will not."

Susan had no answer to make to this strange sentence. She stood, brush in hand, gazing bewilderingly at Ruth's face for a moment. Then, recollecting herself, turned toward the mirror again, with the simple repeatal:

"I beg your pardon. I did not mean to hurt your feelings."

As for Ruth, it would have been difficult for her to analyze her feelings. Were they hurt? Was she angry? If so, at what or whom? Her heart felt in a tumult.

Now, I want you to understand that, strange as it may appear, this was a new question to her. That Judge Burnham was not a Christian man she knew, and regretted. But, that it should affect her answer to his question was a thought which had not once presented itself. She turned and went out from that room without another word, and feeling that she never wanted to say any more words to that girl.

"It is no use," she said, aloud and angrily. "We can never be anything to each other, and it is folly to try. We are set in different molds. I no sooner try to make a friend and confidant of her than some of her tiresome notions crop out and destroy it all."

She knew that all this was nonsense. She knew it was the working of conscience on her own heart that was at this moment making her angry; and yet she found the same relief which possibly you and I have felt in blaming somebody for something, aloud, even while our hearts gainsayed our words.

It is not my purpose to linger over this part of Ruth Erskine's history. The time has come to go on to other scenes. But in this chapter I want to bridge the way, by a word or two of explanation, so that you may the better understand Ruth's mood, and the governing principle of her actions, in the days that followed.

By degrees she came to a quieter state of mind — not, however, until the formalities of the new relation were arranged, and Judge

Burnham had become practically almost one of the family. She grew to realizing that it was a strange, perhaps an unaccountable thing that she, a Christian, should have chosen for her life-long friend and hourly companion one who was really hardly a believer in the Christ to whom she had given herself. She grew to feeling that if this thought had come first, before that promise was made, perhaps she ought to have made a different answer. But I shall have to confess that she drew in with this thought a long breath of relief as she told herself it was settled now. There was no escape from promises as solemn as those which had passed between them; that such covenants were, doubtless, in God's sight, as sacred as the marriage relation itself, and she was glad, to the depths of her soul, that she believed this reasoning to be correct.

At the same time there was a curious sensation of aversion toward the one who had, as it seemed to her, rudely disturbed the first flush of her happiness. The glamour was gone from it all. Henceforth a dull pain, a sense of want, a questioning as to whether she was just where she should be, came in with all the enjoyment

as she struggled with the temptation to feel vindictive toward this disturber of her peace. Besides this, she confided to Judge Burnham the fact that Susan thought she was doing wrong in engaging herself to a man who was not a Christian; and, while he affected to laugh over 't good-naturedly, as a bit of fanaticism which would harm no one, and which was the result of her narrow-minded life hitherto, it meant more than that to him — jarred upon him — and Ruth could see that it did. It affected, perhaps insensibly, his manner toward the offending party. He was not as "brotherly" as he had designed being; and altogether, Susan, since the change was to come, did not regret that Judge Burnham's disposition was to hurry it with all possible speed. Life was less pleasant to her now than it had been any time since her entrance into this distinguished family. The pleasant little blossom of tenderness which had seemed to be about to make itself fragrant for her sister and herself had received a rude blast, and was likely to die outright.

During the weeks that followed there were other developments which served to startle Ruth as hardly anything had done hitherto. They can best be explained by giving you the substance of a conversation between Judge Burnham and herself.

'I ought to tell you something," he said, and the brief sentence was preceded and followed by a pause of such length, and by such evident embarrassment, that Ruth's laugh had a tinge of wonder in it, as she said, "Then, by all means I hope you will do so."

"I suppose it is not altogether new to you?" he said, inquiringly. "Your father has doubtless told you somewhat of my past life."

She shook her head. "Absolutely nothing, save that you were, like himself, a lawyer, resident in the city during term-time, and having a country-seat somewhere. He didn't seem to be very clear as to that. Where is it? I think I shall be glad to live in the country. I never tried it, but I have an idea that it must be delightful to get away from the tumult of the city. Do you enjoy it?"

Judge Burnham's unaccountable embarrassment increased. "You wouldn't like my country-seat," he said decidedly. "I never mean you to see it, if it can be helped. There is a long story connected with it, and with that part of my life. I am sorry that it is entirely new to you; the affair will be more difficult for you to comprehend. May I ask you if you mean you are *utterly* ignorant of my early life? Is it unknown to you that I have once been a married man?"

There was no mistaking the start and the flush of surprise, if it was no deeper feeling, that Ruth exhibited. But she answered quietly enough:

"I am entirely ignorant of your past history, viewed in any phase."

Judge Burnham drew a heavy sigh.

"I said the story was a long one, but I can make it very brief." He began: "You know that a life-time of joy, or misery can be expressed in one sentence. Well, I married when I was a boy; married in haste and repented at leisure, as many a boy has. My wife died when we had been living together for five years, and I have two daughters. They are almost women, I suppose, now. The oldest is seventeen, and they live at the place which you call my country-seat.

Now, these are the headlines of the story. Perhaps you could imagine the rest better than I can tell you. The filling out would take hours, and would be disagreeable both to you and to me. I trust you will let me relieve you from the trial of hearing. There is one thing I specially desire to say to you before this conversation proceeds further: that is, I supposed, of course, you were familiar with these outlines, at least so far as my marriage is concerned, else I should have told you long ago. I have not meant to take any unfair advantage of you. I had not an idea that I was doing so."

"Does my father know that you have daughters?" This was Ruth's question, and her voice, low and constrained, sounded so strangely to herself that she remembered noticing it even then.

"I do not know. It is more than probable that he does not. Indeed, I am not sure that any acquaintance of mine in the city knows this part of my history. My married life was isolated from them all. I have not attempted to conceal it, and, at the same time, I have made no effort to tell it. I am painfully conscious of how all this must look to you, yet I know you will believe that I intended no deception. With regard to the — to my daughters, my professional life has kept me from them almost constantly, so that no idea of *our* home — yours and mine — is associated with them. I have no intention of burying you in the country, and indeed my errand here at this hour was to talk with you in regard to the merits of two hotels, at either of which we can secure desirable rooms."

He hurried over this part of his sentence in a nervous way, as one who was trying, by a rapid change of subject, to turn the current of thought. Ruth brought him back to it with a question which stabbed him.

"But, Judge Burnham, what sort of a father can you have been all these years?" He flushed and paled under it, and under the steadiness of her gaze.

"I — I have hardly deserved the name of father, I suppose, and yet in some respects I have tried to do what it seemed to me I could. Ruth, you don't understand the situation. You think you do, and it looks badly to you, but there are circumstances which make it a peculiarly trying one. However, they are not circumstances which need to touch *you*. I meant and I mean to shield you from all these trials. I asked you to be, not my housekeeper, not a care-taker of two girls who would be utterly uncongenial to you, but my *wife*, and —"

She interrupted him. "And do you suppose, Judge Burnham, that you and I can settle down to a life together of selfish enjoyment in each others' society, ignoring the claims which your children have on you, and which, assuredly, if I become your wife, they *will have* on me? Could you respect me if I were willing to do so?"

It was clear that Judge Burnham was utterly confounded. He arose and stood confronting her, for she had risen to draw aside a fire-screen, and had not, in speaking, resumed her seat. "You do not understand," he muttered, at last. "I have meant nothing wrong. I provide for them, and am willing to do so. I see that they are taken care of; I do not propose to desert them, but it would be simply preposterous to think of burying you up there in the country with that sort of companionship! You do not know what you are talking about. I have never for a moment, thought of such a thing."

"Then it is clearly time to think. If I do not understand *you*, Judge Burnham, neither do you understand me. My life has been anything but a perfect one, or a happy one. I have gone so far wrong myself that it ill becomes me to find fault with others. But there is one thing I will never do. I will never come between a father and his children, separating them from the place which they ought to have beside him Never!"

CHAPTER XVII.

DUTY'S BURDEN.

BY degrees Judge Burnham began to understand the woman whom he had chosen for his wife. Hitherto he had been in the habit of being governed by his own will, of bending forces to his strong purposes. Those occasional characters with whom he came in contact, who refused to be molded by him, he had good-naturedly let alone, crossing their path as little as possible, and teaching himself to believe that they were not worth managing, which was the sole reason why he did not manage them. But Ruth Erskine was a new experience — she *would do* what she believed to be the right thing; and she *would not* yield her convictions to be governed by his judgment. He could not manage *her*, and he had no wish to desert her. Clearly one of them must yield. The entire affair served to keep him in a perturbed state of mind.

Ruth grew more settled. Weeks went by, and her decisions were made, her plans formed, and she walked steadily toward their accomplishment. Not realizing it herself, she was yet engaged in making a compromise with her conscience. She believed herself, perhaps, to have done wrong in promising to become the wife of a man who ignored the principle which governed her life. She would not give back that promise, but she would make the life one of self-abnegation, instead of — what for one brief week it had seemed to her — a resting place, full of light. She would be his wife, but she would also be the mother of his daughters; she would live with them, for them; give up her plans, her tastes, her pursuits, for their sake. In short, she would assume the martyr's garb in good earnest now, and wear it for a lifetime. The more repulsive this course seemed to her — and

it grew very repulsive indeed — the more stead
ily she clung to it; and it was not obstinacy,
you are to understand. It will do for such as
Judge Burnham to call such resolves by that
name; but you should know that Ruth Erskine
was all the time governed by a solemn sense of
duty. It was *cross*, hard, cold, unlightened by
any gleams of peace ; but for all that it started
in a sense of *duty*.

By degrees the "long story," much of it,
came to light — rather was dragged to light —
by a persistent method of cross-questioning
which drove Judge Burnham to the very verge
of desperation.

"Judge Burnham," she would begin, "how
have your daughters been cared for all these
years?"

"Why," he said, wriggling and trying to get
away from his own sense of degradation, "they
had good care; at least I supposed it was.
During their childhood their mother's sister lived
there, and took the sole charge of them. She
was a kind-hearted woman enough, and did her
duty by them."

"But she died, you told me, when they were still children."

"Yes, that was when I was abroad. You see when I went I expected to return in a year at most, but I staid on, following one perplexing tangle after another in connection with my business affairs, until four or five years slipped away. Meantime their aunt died, and the old housekeeper, who had lived with their family since the last century sometime, took her place, and managed for them as well as she could. I didn't realize how things were going. I imagined everything would come out right, you know."

"I don't see how they could," Ruth said, coldly, and Judge Burnham answered nothing.

"Didn't they attend school?"

"Why, yes, they went to the country school out there, you know, when there was one. It is too near the city to secure good advantages, and yet too far away for convenience. I meant, you see, to have them in town, when I came home, at the best schools, and boarding with me, but I found it utterly impracticable — utterly so. You have no conception of what five years of absence will do for people."

"I can imagine something of what five years of neglect would do."

Ruth said it icily — as she *could* speak. Then he would say, "Oh, Ruth!" in a tone which was entreating and almost pitiful. And he would start up and pace back and forth through the room for a moment, until brought back by one of her stabbing questions.

"How have they lived since your return?"

"Why, right here, just where they always have lived. It is the only home they have ever known."

"And they are entirely alone?"

"Why, no. The housekeeper, of whom I told you, had a daughter, a trustworthy woman, and when her mother died this daughter moved to the house, with her family, and has taken care of them."

"And so, Judge Burnham, your two daughters have grown to young ladyhood, isolated from companionship, and from education, and from refinements of every sort, even from their own father, and have been the companions of ignorant hirelings!"

"I tell you, Ruth, you must see them before

you can understand this thing," he would exclaim, in almost despair.

"I assuredly mean to," would be her quiet answer, which answer drove him nearer to desperation than he was before. At last he came and stood before her.

"You force me to speak plainly," he said. "I would have shielded you forever, and you will not let me. These girls are not like your class of girls. They have no interest in refined pursuits. They have no refinement of feeling or manner. They have no desire for education. They do not even care to keep their persons in ordinarily tasteful attire. They care nothing for the refinements of home. They belong to a lower order of being. It is simply impossible to conceive of them as my children; and it is utterly preposterous to think of your associating with them in any way."

She was stilled at last — stunned, it would seem — for she sat in utter silence for minutes that seemed to him hours, while he stood before her and waited. When at last she spoke, her voice was not so cold as it had been, but it was controlled and intensely grave.

"And yet, Judge Burnham, they *are* your children, and you are bound to them by the most solemn and sacred vows which it is possible for a man to take on his lips. How can you ever hope to escape a just reward for ignoring them? Now, I must tell you what I feel and mean. I do not intend to be hard or harsh, and yet I intend to be true. I am not sure that I am acting or talking as other girls would, under like circumstances; but that is a question which has never troubled me. I am acting in what I believe to be the right way. You have asked me to be your wife, and I have promised in good faith. It was before I knew any of this story, which, in a sense, alters the ground on which we stood. I will tell you plainly what I believe I ought to do, and what, with my present views, I *must* do. I will give my life to helping you in this matter. I will go up to that home of yours and hide myself with those girls, and we will both do what we can to retrieve the mistakes of a lifetime. I will struggle and plan and endure for them. I am somewhat versed in the duties which this sort of living involves, as you know, and in the crosses which it brings. Perhaps it was for this reason they were sent to me. I have chafed under them, and been weak and worthless, God knows; and yet I feel that perhaps he is giving me another chance. I will try to do better work for him, in your home, than I have in my own. At any rate, I *must try*. If I fail, it shall be after the most solemn and earnest efforts that I can make. But, as I said, it *must be* tried. This is not all self-sacrifice, Judge Burnham. I mean that I could not do it, would not see that I had any right to do it, if I had not given my heart to *you;* and if for the love of you I could not trust myself to help you in *your* duty. But you must fully understand that it seems unquestionably to be your duty. You must not shirk it; I must never help you to shirk it; I should not dare. I will go with you to that home, and be with you a member of that family. But I can never make with you another home that does not include the *family.* I *must never do it.*"

Judge Burnham hoped to turn her away from this decision, which was, to him, simply an awful one! Do you imagine that he accomplished it? I believe you know her better. It is necessary for you to remember that he did not understand the underlying motive by which she was governed. When she said, "I *must* not do it," he did not understand that she meant her vows to Christ would not let her. He believed, simply, that she set her judgment above his, in this matter, and determined that she *would* not yield it. The struggle was a severe one. At times he felt as though he would say to her, if she "*must* not" share with him the home he had so lovingly and tenderly planned for her, why, then, *he* must give her up. The only reason that he did not say this, was because he did not dare to try it. He had not the slightest intention of giving her up; and he was afraid she would take him at his word, as assuredly she would have done. She was dearer to him, in her obstinacy, than anything in life — and nothing must be risked. Therefore was he sore beset; and, as often as he renewed the struggle, he came off worsted. How could it be otherwise, when Ruth could constantly flee back to that unanswerable position — "Judge Burnham, it is *wrong;* I *must* not do it?" What if *he* didn't understand her? He saw that she understood herself, and meant what she said.

So it came to pass that, as the days went by, and the hour for the marriage drew nearer and nearer, Judge Burnham felt the plans, so dear to his heart, slipping away from under his control. Ruth would be *married*. Well, that was a great point gained. But she would not go away for a wedding journey; she would not go to the Grand Hotel, where he desired to take rooms — no, not for a day, or hour. She would not have the trial of contrast between the few, first bright days of each other, and the dismal days following, when they had each other, with something constantly coming between. She would go directly to that country home, and nowhere else She would go to it just as it was. He was not to alter the surroundings or the outward life, in one single respect. She meant to see the home influence which had molded those girls exactly as it had breathed about them, without any outside hand to change it. She proposed to do the changing herself. One little bit of compromise her stern conscience admitted — her future husband might fit up one room for her use — her private retreat — according to his individual taste, and she would accept it from him as hers. But the outer life, that was to be lived as a family, he must not touch.

"But Ruth," he said, "you do not understand. Things have utterly gone to decay. There was no one to care, or appreciate; there was no one to *take* care of anything, and I let everything go."

"Very well," she said; "then we will see what our united tastes can do, toward setting everything right, when we come to feel what is wanted."

"Then couldn't you go with me and see the place, a few weeks before we go there, and give directions, such as you would like to see carried out?—just a few, you know, such as you can take in at a glance, to make it a little more like home?"

She shook her head decidedly. No, indeed. She was not going there to spy out the desolation of the land. She was going to it as a *home;* and if, as a home, it was defective, together they — he, his daughters and herself — would see what was needed, and remodel it.

How dismally he shook his head over that!

He knew his daughters, and she did not. He tried again :

"But, Ruth, it is five miles from the railroad. How will it be possible to ride ten miles by train, and five by carriage, night and morning. and attend to business?"

"Easily," she said, quietly; "except in term-time. The busiest season that my father ever had we were in the country, and he came out nearly every evening. In term-time we must *all* come into town and board, I suppose."

He winced over this, and was silent, and felt himself giving up his last hope of holding this thing in check, and began to realize that he loved this future wife of his very much indeed, else he could never submit to such a state of things. He believed it would last for but a little while — just long enough for her to see the hopelessness of things. But this "seeing," with her, into all its hopelessness, was what he shrank from.

So the days went by; not much joy in them for any one concerned. Away from Ruth's influence, Judge Burnham was annoyed, to such a degree, that he could hardly make a civil answer to the most ordinary question; and his office clerks grumbled among themselves that, if it made such a bear of a man to know that in three weeks he was to have a wife, they hoped their turn would never come. Away from his presence, Ruth was grave to a degree that threw an added shadow over the home-life. Susan felt herself to be in disgrace with her sister, and had been unable thus far, to rise above it, and be helpful, as she would have liked to be. Judge Erskine, hearing more details from his friend than from his daughter, sympathized with her strong sense of duty, honored her, rejoiced in her strength of purpose, and was *sorry* for her, realizing, more than before, what a continuous chain of trial her life had been of late. Therefore, his tone was tender and sympathizing, when he spoke to her, but sad, as one who felt *too* deeply, and was not able to impart strength.

As for Mrs. Erskine, she had so much to say about the strangeness of it all — wondering how Judge Burnham could have managed to keep things so secret, and how the girls looked, whether they favored him, or their ma, and whether they would be comfortable sort of persons to get along with — that Ruth was driven to the very verge of distraction, and felt, at times, that, to get out of that house, into any other on earth, would be a relief.

There was much ado, also, about that wedding. Mrs. Erskine wanted marvelous things — an illumination, and a feast, and a crowd, and all the resources of the rain-bow, as to bridal toilet. But here, as in other matters, Ruth held steadily to her own way, and brought it to pass — a strictly private wedding, in the front parlor of her father's house; not a person, outside of the Erskine family circle, to witness the ceremony, save Marion Dennis; she, by virtue of being Dr. Dennis' wife, gained admission. But Marion Dennis' tears fell fast behind the raised handkerchief, which shielded her face during the solemn prayer. She knew, in detail, some of Ruth's plans. She knew, better than Ruth did -- so *she* thought — that plans are sometimes hard to carry out. How many *she* had indulged' and, at this moment, there sat at home, her haughty daughter, Grace, entirely unforgiving, because of *her* "meddling" — so she styled the earnest attempts to shield her from danger. To Marion, Ruth's future had never looked less hopeful than it did on this marriage morning.

It may be that her own disappointments caused some of the flowing tears; but her *heart* ached for Ruth. What should *she* do without a Christian husband — a husband entirely in sympathy with every effort, and entirely tender with every failure of hers! What was Ruth to do, with Judge Burnham for a husband, instead of Dr. Dennis! How were the trials of life to be borne with any man living except this *one!*

Thus reasoned silly Marion — unconsciously, indeed; but that was as it seemed to her.

Well for Ruth, that even at this moment, she could look into the face of the man whom she had chosen, and feel: "It is after all, for *him.* There is no other person for whom I could begin this life."

Said a friend, the other day, in sympathetic tones, as she spoke of a young bride going far from her home and her mother: "I feel so sorry for her. It is such a trying experience, all alone, away from all her early friends."

"But," I said, "after all, she doesn't go as

far as you told me you did, when you were married."

The answer was quick:

"Oh, no; but then I had *my husband,* you know; and she — "

And then she stopped to laugh.

So it was a blessed thing that Ruth Burnham, going out from the home which had sheltered her, felt that she went *with her husband.*

CHAPTER XVIII.

EMBARRASSMENT AND MERRIMENT.

SUPPOSE there was never a bride going out from her home, with her husband, who was more silent than was our Ruth. It was the silence of constraint, too. It was such a little journey! ten miles or so, by train, then five by carriage, and then — what *were* they coming to? If only it had been her husband's happy home, where treasures were waiting to greet him, and be clasped to his heart, Ruth felt that it would have been *so* much easier.

Yet I think, very likely, she did not understand her own heart. Probably the easiest excuse that we can make for ourselves, or for our shrinking from duties, is, " If it were *only* something else, I could do it." I think it quite likely that had Ruth been going to just such a home as she imagined would make her cross lighter, she would have been jealous of those clasping hands and tender kisses. The human heart is a strange instrument, played upon in all sorts of discords, even when we think there is going to be music. As it was, the certainty of her husband's disapproval, the sense of strangeness, and the sense of shrinking from the new trials, and the questioning as to whether, after all, she had done right, all served to depress Ruth's heart and hush her voice, to such a degree that she felt speech was impossible. I want to linger a minute over one sentence — the questioning as to whether, after all, she had done right. There is no more miserable state of mind than this. It is such dreadful ground for the *Christian* to occupy! Yet, practically, half the Christians in the world are there. Theoretically, we believe ourselves to be led, even in the common affairs of life, by the All-wise Spirit of God; theoretically, we believe that *He* can make no mistake; theoretically, we believe that it is just as easy to get an answer from that Spirit — "a word behind thee," as the Bible phrases it, directing us which way to go — as it is to hear our human friend answer to our call. But, practically, what *do* we believe? What is the reason that so much of our life is given up to mourning over *possible* mistakes? Is it because we choose to decide some questions for ourselves without bringing them to the test of prayer? or because, having asked for direction, we failed to watch for the answer, or expect it, and so lost the "still small voice?" Or is it, sometimes, because having heard the voice, we regret its direction and turn from it, and choose our own?

Ruth Burnham was conscious of none of these states. She had prayed over this matter; indeed, it seemed to her that she had done little else than pray, of late; and, in some points, she was strong, feeling that her feet had been set upon a rock. But in others there was, at this too late moment, a sense of faltering. "Might she not," asked her conscience of her, "have yielded somewhat? Would it have worked any ill for them both to have gone away from everybody for a few weeks, as Judge Burnham so desired to do, and have learned to know and help each other, and have learned to talk freely together about this new home, and have grown stronger together, before facing this manifest duty?"

I do not tell you she might have done all this. Perhaps her first position, that it would have been unwise and unhelpful, was the right one. I think we do, sometimes, put added touches of our own to the cross that the Father lays upon us, making it shade in gloom, when he would have tinted it with the sunlight. But I do not say that Ruth had done this. I don't know which was wise. What I *am* sure of is, that she, having left it to Christ; having asked for his direction, and having received it (for unless she thought she had been shown the step to take, assured she ought not to have stepped,) she had no right to unrest herself and strap on to her heart the burden of that wearying question, "*Did* I, after all, do right?"

Judge Burnham could match her in quietness. He had her beside him at last. She was his wife; she bore his name; henceforth their in terests were one, Thus much of what he had months ago set himself steadily to accomplish had been accomplished. But not a touch of the details was according to his plans. The situation in which he found himself was so new and so bewildering, that while he meant, for her sake, to make the best of it until such time as she should see that she was wrong and he right, yet, truth to tell, he hardly knew how to set about making the best of it.

He did what he could. No topic for conversation that suggested itself to his mind seemed entirely safe. And, beside, what use to try to converse for so short a journey? So he contented himself with opening her car-window, and dropping her blind, and arranging her travelling-shawl comfortably for a shoulder-support, and in other nameless, thoughtful ways making this bit of a journey bright with care-taking tenderness. It served to show Ruth how royally he would have cared for her in the longer journey which he wanted, and which she wouldn't have. Whereupon she immediately said to her heart "Perhaps it would have been better if I had yielded." And that made her miserable. There was no time to yield now. The station was called out, and there was bustle and haste and no little nervousness in getting off in time, for the train seemed, before it fairly halted, to have been sorry for that attempt at accommodation, and began to show signs of going on again that were nerve-distracting. It annoyed Judge Burnham to the degree that he said, savagely, to the conductor, "It was hardly worth while to stop, if you can't do it more comfortably." He would have liked so much to have been leisurely and comfortable; to have done everything in a composed, travelled manner; he understood so thoroughly all the details of travelled life. Why *could* he not show Ruth some of the comforts of it? That little station! It was in itself a curiosity to Ruth. She had not supposed, that ten miles away from a city, anything could be so diminutive. A long, low, unpainted building, with benches for seats, and loungers spitting tobacco-juice for furniture. There was evidently something unusual to stare at. This was the presence of a quiet, tasteful carriage, with handsome horses, and a driver who indicated, by the very flourish of his whip, that this was a new locality to him. He and his horses and his carriage belonged, unmistakably, to city-life, and had rarely reached so far out.

"Is this your carriage?" Ruth asked, surveying it with a touch of satisfaction as Judge Burnham made her comfortable among the cushions.

"No, it is from town. There are no carriages belonging to this enlightened region."

"How do your family reach the station, then?"

"They never reach it," he answered, composedly. He had resolved upon not trying to smooth over anything.

"But how did you get to and from the cars when you were stopping here?"

"On the rare occasions when I was so unfortunate as to stop here I sometimes caught the wagon which brings the mail and takes unfortunate passengers; or, if I were too early for that, there were certain milk-carts and vegetable-carts which gave me the privilege of a ride, with a little persuasion in the shape of money."

Nothing could be more studiedly polite than Judge Burnham's tone; but there was a covert sarcasm in every word he said. He seemed to Ruth to be thinking, "I hope you realize the uncomfortable position into which your obstinacy has forced me."

Evidently not a touch of help was to be had from him. What were they to talk about during that five miles of travel over a rough road? Ruth studied her brains to try to develop a subject that would not make them even more uncomfortable than they now felt. She was unfortunate in selection, but it seemed impossible to get away from the thoughts which were just now so prominently before them. She suddenly remembered a fact which surprised her, and to which she gave instant expression.

"Judge Burnham, what are your daughter's names?"

The gentleman thus addressed wrinkled his forehead into a dozen frowns, and shook himself, as though he would like to shake away all remembrance of the subject, before he said:

"Their very names are a source of mortification to me. The elder is Seraphina and the other Araminta. What do you think of them?"

Ruth was silent and dismayed. This apparently trivial circumstance served to show her what a strange state of things existed in the home whither she was going. She didn't know how to answer her husband's question. She was sorry that she had asked any. There seemed no way out but to ask another, which, in truth, pressed upon her.

"How do you soften such names? What do you call them when you address them?"

"I call them nothing. I know of no way of smoothing such hopeless cognomens, and I take refuge in silence, or bewildering pronouns."

Ruth pondered over this answer long enough to have her courage rise and to grow almost indignant. Then she spoke again:

"But, Judge Burnham, I do not see how you could have allowed so strange a selection for girls in this age of the world. Why didn't you save them from such a life-long infliction? Or, was there some reason for the use of these names that dignifies them — that makes them sacred?"

"There is this sole reason for the names, and for many things which you will find yourself unable to understand. Their mother was a hopeless victim to fourth-rate sensation novels, and named her daughters from that standpoint. I was in reality powerless to interfere. You may have discovered before this that I am not always able to follow out the dictates of my own judgment, and others, as well as myself, have to suffer in consequence."

What could Ruth answer to this? She felt its covert meaning; and so sure was she beginning to feel that she had followed her own ideas, instead of the leadings of any higher voice, that she had not the heart to be offended with the plainness of the insinuation. But she realized that it was a strange conversation for a newly-made husband and wife. She took refuge again in silence. Judge Burnham tried to talk. He asked if the seat she occupied was entirely comfortable, and if she enjoyed riding, and if she had tried the saddle, or thought she would enjoy such exercise, and presently he said:

"These are abominable roads. I am sorry to have you so roughly treated in the very beginning of our journey together. I did not want roughness to come to you, Ruth. I thought that you had endured enough.

She was sorry that he said this. Her tears were never nearer the surface than at this moment, and she did not want to shed them. She began to talk rapidly to him about the beauty of the far-away hills which stretched bluely before them, and he tried to help her effort and appreciate them. Still it was too apparent just then neither cared much for hills; and it was almost a relief when the carriage at last drew up under a row of elms. These, at least, were beautiful. So was the long, irregular, grassy yard that stretched away up the hill, and was shaded by noble old trees. It required but a moment to dismiss the carriage, and then her husband gave her his arm, and together they toiled up the straggling walk toward the long, low building, which was in dire need of paint.

"This yard is lovely," Ruth said, and she wondered if her voice trembled very much.

"I used to like the yard, a hundred years or so ago," he answered sadly. "It really seems to me almost as long ago as that since I had any pleasant recollections of anything connected with it."

"Was it your mother's home?"

"Yes," he said, and his face grew tender. "And she was a good mother, Ruth; I loved the old house once for her sake."

"I think I can make you love it again for mine." Ruth said the words gently, with a tender intonation that was very pleasant to hear, and that not many people heard from her. Judge Burnham was aware of it, and his grave face brightened a little. He reached after her hand, and held it within his own, and the pressure he gave it said what he could not speak. So they went up the steps of that low porch with lighter hearts, after all, than had seemed possible.

The door at the end of that porch opened directly into the front room, or "keeping room," as, in the parlance of that region of country, it was called, though Ruth did not know it. The opening of that door was a revelation to her. She had never been in a real country room before. There were green paper shades to the windows, worn with years, and faded; and little twinkling rays of the summer sunshine pushed in through innumerable tiny holes, which holes, curiously enough, Ruth saw and remembered, and associated forever after with that hour and moment. There was a rag carpet on the floor, of dingy colors and uneven weaving. Ruth did not even know the name of that style of carpet, but she knew it was peculiar. There were cane-seated chairs, standing in solemn rows at proper intervals. There was a square table or "stand," if she had but known the proper name for it, covered with a red cotton cloth having a gay border and fringed edges. There was a wooden chair or two, shrinking back from contact with the "smarter" cane-seated ones; and there was a large, old-fashioned, high-backed wooden rocker, covered back and arms and sides, with a gay patch-work cover, aglow with red and green and yellow, and it seemed, to poor Ruth, a hundred other dazzling colors, and the whole effect reminded her forcibly of Mrs. Judge Erskine!

Now, you have a list of every article of furniture which this large room contained. No, I forget the mantle-piece, though Ruth did not. It was long and deep and high, and was adorned with a curious picture or two, which would bear studying before you could be sure what they were, and with two large, bright, brass candlesticks, and a tray and snuffers. Also, in the center, a fair-sized kerosene lamp, which looked depraved enough to smoke like a furnace, without even waiting to be lighted! Also, there were some oriental paintings in wooden frames on the wall. Are you so fortunate as not to understand what oriental paintings are? Then you will be unable to comprehend a description of Ruth's face as her eye rested on them! Judge Burnham was looking at her as her eye roved swiftly and silently over this scene, not excepting the curious paper, with which the walls were hung in a pattern long gone by. He stood a little at one side, affecting to raise an unmanageable window sash. They were all unmanageable; but in reality he was watching her, and I must confess to you that this scene, contrasted in his mind with the elegant home which his wife had left, was fast taking a ludicrous side to him. The embarrassments were great, and he knew that they would thicken upon him, and yet the desire to laugh overcame all other emotions. His eyes danced, and he bit his lips to restrain their mirth. But at last, when Ruth turned and looked at him, the expression in her face overcame him, and he burst forth **into** laughter.

It was a blessed thing for Ruth that she was able to join him.

"Sit down," he said, wheeling the gay rocker toward her. "I am sure you never occupied so elegant a seat before. There is a great gray cat belonging to the establishment who usually sits in state here, but she has evidently vacated in your favor to-day."

Ruth sank into the chair, unable to speak; the strangeness of it all, and the conflicting emotions stirring in her heart fairly took away the power of speech. Judge Burnham came and stood beside her.

"We have entered into this thing, Ruth," he said, and his voice was not so hard as it had been, "and there are embarrassments enough certainly connected with it, and yet it is a home, and it is *our* home — yours and mine — and we are *together forever*. This, of itself, is joy enough to atone for almost anything."

She was about to answer him, and there was a smile on her face, in the midst of tears in her eyes; but they were interrupted. The door opened suddenly, and an apparition in the shape of a child, perhaps five years old, appeared to them — a tow-headed child with staring blue eyes and wide-open mouth — a child in a very pink dress, not over-clean and rather short, — a child with bare feet, and with her arms full of a great gray cat. She stared amazingly at them for a moment, then turned and vanished.

"*That* is not mine, at least," Judge Burnham said, and the tone in which he said it was irresistible.

His eyes met Ruth's at that moment, and all traces of tears had disappeared, also all signs of sentiment. There was but one thing to do, and they did it; and the old house rang with peal after peal of uncontrollable laughter.

CHAPTER XIX.

MY DAUGHTERS.

THE room to which Judge Burnham presently escorted his bride was very unlike that parlor. As she looked about her, on the exquisite air of beauty which prevailed, and the evidences of refined and cultured taste, scattered with lavish hand, she was touched with the thought that her tastes had been understood and remembered, in each minute detail.

"How very lovely this is!" she said, as her foot rested on the soft velvet carpet, with its wildwood vines trailing in rich colors over the floor.

"I knew you would like it," Judge Burnham

said, with a gratified smile. "It reminded me of you, and, indeed, the entire room has seemed to me to be full of your presence. I enjoyed arranging it. I think I could have gratified your tastes in regard to the rest of the house, Ruth, if you had let me."

"Oh, I know you could," she answered, earnestly. "It was not that I did not trust your taste — and perhaps I made a mistake; but I meant it right, and you must help me to bring right out of it."

She did not realize it, but this little concession to his possible better judgment helped her husband wonderfully.

"We will make it come right," he said, decidedly. "And now I will leave you to rest a little, while I go down and discover whether this house is inhabited to-day."

With the door closing after him seemed to go much of Ruth's courage. This exquisite room was a rest to her beauty-loving eyes and heart. But it contrasted most strangely with the life below stairs; and, when she thought of that room below, it reminded her of all there was yet to meet and endure, and of the newness of the way, and the untried experiments which were to be made, and of her own weakness — and her heart trembled, and almost failed her. Yet it must not fail her; she *must* get strength.

Well for Ruth that she knew in what place to seek it. Instead of taking a seat in the delicately-carved and gracefully-upholstered easy-chair, which invited her into its depths, she turned and knelt before it. Perhaps, after all, there are more dangerous experiences than those which, in coming to a new home, to take up new responsibilities, lead us to feel our utter weakness, and bring us on our knees, crying to the strong for strength.

Judge Burnham's entrance, nearly an hour afterward, found Ruth resting quietly in that easy chair, such a calm on her face, and such a light in her eyes, that he stopped on the threshold, and regarded her with a half-pleased, half-awed expression, as he said:

"You look wonderfully rested! I think my easy chair must be a success. Will you come down now, to a farm-house supper? Please don't see any more of the strange things than you can help. I tried to get the girls to come up, and so avoid some of the horrors of a meeting below stairs; but they are too thoroughly alarmed to have any sense at all, and I had to abandon that plan."

"Poor things!" said Ruth, compassionately. "Am I so very formidable? It must be dreadful to feel frightened at people. I can't imagine the feeling."

He surveyed her critically, then laughed. He had some conception of what a vision she would be to the people down-stairs. She had not changed her travelling dress, which was of rich dark silk, fitted exquisitely to her shapely form, and the soft laces at throat and wrist, brightened only by a knot of ribbon of the most delicate tint of blue, completed what, to Judge Burnham's cultured taste, seemed the very perfection of a toilet.

"You do not frighten me," he said. "I can manage to look at you without being overwhelmed. I shall not answer for anybody else. Ruth, I have obeyed you to the very letter. In a fit of something very like vexation, I resolved not to lift a finger to change the customs of the house, leaving you to see them, according to your desire, as they were. The result is we haven't even a table to ourselves, to-night. The whole of that insufferable family, cat and all, are ready to gather, with us, around their hospitable board. I am sorry, now, that I was so very literal in my obedience."

"I am not," Ruth said, and her tone was quiet, and had a sound in it which was not there when he left her. It served to make him regard her again, curiously.

Then they went down-stairs to the kitchen! Ruth was presently seated at the long table, alarmingly near to the stove which had cooked the potatoes that graced the evening meal — boiled potatoes, served in their original coats! to be eaten with two-tined steel forks, the same forks expected to do duty in the mastication of a huge piece of peach-pie!— unless, indeed, she did as her husband's daughters were evidently accustomed to doing, and ate it with her knife. There were, at that table, Farmer Ferris, in his shirt-sleeves, himself redolent of the barn and the cow-house; his wife, in a new, stiff, blue and red plaid calico, most manifestly donned to do honor to the occasion; two boys, belonging to the

Ferris household, in different degrees of shock headed, out-at-the-elbow disorder, and the afore said apparition in pink calico, the gray cat still hugged to her heart, and eating milk from the same saucer, at intervals; and, lastly, the two daughters of the House of Burnham.

Those daughters! The strongest emotion which Ruth found it in her heart to have for them, on this first evening, was pity. She had never imagined anything like the painful embarrassment which they felt. They sat on the edges of their chairs, and, when engaged in trying to eat, tilted the chairs forward to reach their plates, and rested their elbows on the table to stare, when they dared to raise their frightened eyes to do so. Their father had performed the ceremony of introduction in a way which was likely to increase their painful self-consciousness. "Girls," he had said, and his voice sounded as if he were summoning them to a trial by jury; "this is Mrs. Burnham." And they had stood up, and essayed to make little bobbing courtesies, after the fashion of fifty years ago, until futher pressed by Mrs. Ferris, who had said, with a conscious laugh:

"For the land's sake, girls! do go and shake hands with her. Why, she is your ma now."

But Judge Burnham's haughty voice had come to the rescue:

"If you please, we will excuse them from that ceremony, Mrs. Ferris," he had said. "Mrs. Burnham, please be seated." And he had drawn back her chair with the courtesy of a gentleman and the inward fury of a lion. In truth, Judge Burnham was ashamed of and angry with himself, and I am glad of it; he deserved to be. Instead of asserting his authority, and making this meeting and this first meal together strictly a family matter, and managing a dozen other little details which he could have managed, and which would have helped wonderfully, he had angrily resolved to let everything utterly alone, and bring Ruth thus sooner and more decisively to seeing the folly, and the utter untenableness of her position. But something in the absolute calm of her face, this evening — a calm which had come to her since he left her in their room alone — made him feel it to be more than probable that she would not easily, nor soon, abandon the position which she had assumed.

The ordeal of supper was gotten through with easier than Ruth had supposed possible — though truth to tell, the things which would have affected most persons the least, were the hardest for her to bear. She had not entirely risen above the views concerning refinement which she had expressed during the early days of Chautauqua life; and to eat with a knife when a fork should be used, and to have a two-tined steel fork, instead of a silver one, and to have no napkin at all, were to her positive and vivid sources of discomfort — sources from which she could not altogether turn away, even at this time. I am not sure, however, that, in the trivialities, she did not lose some of the real trials which the occasion certainly presented.

Directly after the supper was concluded, with but a very poor attempt at eating on Ruth's part, Judge Burnham led the way to that dreadful parlor, interposing his stern voice between the evident intention of the daughters to remain in the kitchen:

"I desire that you will come immediately to the parlor."

As for Ruth and himself, they did not retreat

promptly enough to escape Mrs. Ferris' stage whisper:

"For the land's sake, girls! do go quick; I'm afraid he will bite you next time. I wonder if she is as awful cross as he is? She looks it, and more too."

In the midst of all the tumult of thought which there might have been, Ruth found herself trying to determine which was the most objectional expression of the two, Mrs. Judge Erskine's favorite "Land alive!" or Mrs. Ferris' "For the land's sake!" Where do Americans get their favorite expletives, anyway?

She had not much time to query, for here were these girls, sitting each on the edge of one of the solemn cane-seated chairs, and looking as thorroughly miserable as the most hard-hearted could have desired. What was she to say to them, or would it be more merciful to say nothing at all? Ruth felt an unutterable pity for them. How miserably afraid they were of their father! How entirely unnatural it seemed! And it could not be that he had ever been actually unkind to them? It was just a system of severe letting alone, combined with the unwisdom of the Ferris tongue which had developed such results. Between the intervals of trying to say a few words to them, words which they answered with solemn " Yes, ma'ams," Ruth tried to study their personal appearance. It was far from prepossessing; yet, remembering Susan, and the marvelous changes which the "ivy-green dress," fitted to her form, had accomplished, wondered how much of their painful awkwardness was due to the utter unsuitability of their attire, and the uncouth arrangement of their *coiffures*.

The elder of the two was tall and gaunt, with pale, reddish, yellow hair — an abundance of it, which she seemed to think served no purpose but to annoy her, and was to be stretched back out of the way as far and as tightly as possible. Her shoulders were bent and stooping; her pale, blue eyes looked as though, when they were not full of dismayed embarrassment, they were listless, and her whole manner betokened that of a person who was a trial to herself, and to every one with whom she came in contact.

People, with such forms and faces, almost invariably manage to fit themselves out in clothing which shows every imperfection to advantage. This girl was no exception; indeed, she seemed to have succeeded in making an exceptional fright of herself. Her dress was of the color and material which seemed to increase her height, and bore the marks of a novice in dressmaking about every part of it. To increase the effect it was much too short for her, and showed to immense disadvantage a pair of strong, thick country boots, which might have been excellent for tramping over plowed ground in wet weather. The younger sister was a complete contrast in every respect. Her form can only be described by that expressive and not very elegant word "chunky." From her thick, short hair, down to her thickly-shod feet, she seemed to be almost equally shapeless and graceless; fat, red cheeks; small, round eyes shining out from layers of fat; large, ill-shaped hands; remarkably large feet, apparently, or else her shoes were, and arrayed in a large plaided dress of red and green, which was much too low in the neck and much too short-waisted, and was absolutely uncouth! Swiftly, silently, Ruth took in all these details. And she took in, also, what her husband had never known — that a large portion of this uncouthness was due to the outward adornings or disguisings, which is what persons devoid of taste sometimes succeed in making of their dress.

In the midst of her musings there came to her a new idea. It dawned upon her in the form of a question. Why should she, a lady of fashion and of leisure, and of such cultured taste that she was an acknowledged authority among her friends, on all matters pertaining to the esthetic, be in so marked a manner, for the second time in her short life, brought face to face with that form of ill-breeding which troubled her the most? Not only face to face with it, but put in such a position that it was her duty to endure it patiently and show kindly interest in the victims? Was it possible? And this thought flashed upon her like a revelation — that she had been wont to make too much of this matter; that she had allowed the lack of culture in these directions to press her too sorely. Now, do you know that this was the first time such a possibility had dawned on Ruth Burnham? So insensible had been her yielding to the temptation which wealth and leisure brings, to give too much thought and too high a place to these questions of dress and taste, that, as I say, she had not been conscious of any sin in that direction, while those who looked on at her life had been able to see it plainly, and in exaggerated form!

I suspect, dear friend, that you, at this moment, are the victim of some inconsistency which your next-door neighbor sees plainly, and which, possibly, injures your influence over her, and you are not conscious of its development. Now, that is a solemn thought, as well as a perplexing one, for what is to be done about it? "Cleanse thou me from secret faults," prayed the inspired writer. May he not have meant those faults so secret that it takes the voice of God to reveal them to our hearts?

At least to Ruth Burnham, sitting there in that high-backed rocker, looking at her husband's daughters, the thought came like the voice of God's Spirit in her heart. She had come very near to that revealing Spirit during the last two hours — rather he had made his presence known to her. She was in a hushed mood, desiring to be led, and she plainly saw that even this exhibition of uncouthness could be a discipline to her soul, if she would but allow its voice. You are not to understand that she, therefore, concluded uncouthness and utter disregard of refined tastes to be necessary outgrowths of Christian experience, or to be in the least necessary to a higher development of Christian life. She merely had a glimpse of what it meant, to be in a state of using this world as not abusing it. The thought quickened her resolutions in regard to those neglected girls thus thrown under her care, and, I have no doubt, that it toned her voice when she spoke to them. I believe it not irreverent to say that the very subject upon which she first addressed them was chosen for her, all unconsciously to herself, by that Ever-present Spirit, to whom nothing that an immortal soul can say, appears trivial, because he sees the waves of influence which are stirred years ahead by the quiet words.

Just what the two frightened girls expected from her would have been, perhaps, difficult for even themselves to explain. For years all their intercourse with their father had consisted in a series of irritated lectures, delivered in a sharp key, on his part, and received in a frightened silence by them. He had been utterly disappointed with them in every respect, and he had not failed to show it, and they had not failed to seek for sympathy by pouring the story of their grievances into Mrs. Ferris' willing ears. The result was that she had but increased their terror in and doubt of their father. Added to this, she had all the ignorant superstition of her class in regard to step-mothers, if, indeed the views of this sort of people shall be called by no harsher name than superstition. The new-comer had been, during the last week, most freely discussed in the Ferris household, and the result had been what might have been expected. Therefore, it was with unfeigned amazement and with the demonstrations of prolonged stares, that Ruth's first suddenly spoken sentence broke the silence which the others were feeling keenly.

"Your hair looks as though it would curl, naturally; did you ever try it?"

This to the elder girl, whose whole face reddened under the astonishment produced by the query, and who, as I said, could only stare for a moment. Then she said·

"Yes, ma'am, I did once; long time ago."

"And didn't you like the appearance?"

A more vivid blush and a conscious laugh was the answer. Then she added:

"Why, yes, well enough; but it was such a bother, and nobody to care."

"Oh, it is very little trouble." Mrs. Burnham answered, lightly, "when you understand just how to manage it. I think natural curls are beautiful."

CHAPTER XX.

A SISTER NEEDED.

SOME vigorous planning was done that night which followed Ruth Burnham's introduction to her new home. It was not restless planning; neither could it be said to be about new things, for these things Ruth had studied every day since the first week of her engagement, and the summer, which was in its spring-time then, was fading now, so she had *thought* before. But something had given her thoughts new strength and force. Ruth believed it to be that hour which she had spent alone on her knees. She had spent many an hour before that alone on her knees, but never had the power of the unseen presence taken such hold upon her as at that time. She had felt her own powerlessness as *Ruth Erskine* had not been given to feeling it, and you know it is "man's extremity that is God's opportunity."

It was before the hour of breakfast that she commenced the process of developing some of her plans to her husband.

"How long will it take to dispose of the Ferris family?" she asked him, and her voice was so calm, so full of strength, and conscious determination that it rested him.

"It can be done just as soon as your genius, combined with my executive ability, can bring it to pass," he answered, laughing, "and I sincerely hope and trust that you will be brilliant and rapid in your display of genius."

"But, Judge Burnham, ought they to have warning, as we do with servants?"

"A week's warning? I trust not! I should not promise to endure a week of it. Oh, they are prepared. I broadly hinted to them that the mistress would want the house to herself. If they had not felt the necessity of being here to welcome you it could have been managed before this. They have their plans formed, I believe, and as soon as you want to manage without them, I will make it for their interest to be in haste."

Ruth turned toward him with a relieved smile and an eager air. "Could you manage, then, to make it to their interest to go before breakfast, or shall we have to wait until that meal is over?"

He laughed, gayly. "Your energy is refreshing," he said, "especially when it is bestowed in such a worthy cause. No, I think we will have to wait until after breakfast. But, Ruth, are you really in earnest? Do you actually mean to settle down here, in this house, as it is? And what are you going to do about help, and about -- well, everything?"

Before she answered she came over and stood beside him, slipping her hand through his arm and speaking in tender earnestness. "Judge Burnham, I want you to understand me; I feel that I may have seemed hard, and cold, and selfish. Perhaps I have been selfish in pushing my plan; I think I have been, but I did not intend it for selfishness. I was, and am, led by what seems to be *our* duty — yours and mine.

Those girls of yours have been neglected. I can see how you, being a man, would not know what to do; at the same time I can see how I, being a woman, can at least *try* to do many things, and I am very eager to try. You may call it an experiment if you will, and if it is, in your estimation in six months from now an utter failure, I will give it up and do exactly as you propose."

There was a gleam of assurance in her eyes, and he could see that she did not believe he would ever be called upon to follow *his* plans. But something tender and pleading in her tone touched him, and he said, with feeling:

"I begin to realize forcibly, what has only come upon me in touches heretofore — that I have not done my duty by the girls. I did not know what to do. I used to study the question and try to plan it, but I can not tell you how utterly hopeless it seemed to me. Finally, I gave it up. I determined that nothing could ever be done but to support them and live away from them, and long before I knew you I determined on that as my line of action. So your resolution was a surprise to me — an overwhelming one. But, perhaps, you are right. At least I will help you in whatever way I can to carry out *your* plans, however wild they are, and I begin to realize that you may possibly have some very wild ones, but I promise allegiance."

"Good!" said Ruth, with sparkling eyes, "I ask nothing better than that. Then we will proceed at once to business; there is so much to be done that I don't feel like taking a wedding journey just now. We can enjoy it so much more when we get our house in order. There are certain things that I need to know at once. First, how much or how little is there to be done to this house, and — and to everything? In other words, how much money am I to spend?"

"Oh," he said looking relieved, "I thought you were going to ask me what ought to be done to make the place habitable, and, really, I hardly know where to commence. I shall be charmed to leave it in your hands. As to money, I think I may safely promise you what you need unless your ideas are on a more magnificent scale than I think. I will give you my check this morning for a thousand dollars, and when that is used you may come to me for as much more. Is that an answer to your question?"

"An entirely satisfactory one." She answered him with shining eyes, and they went down to breakfast with a sense of satisfaction which, considering the surroundings and the marvelous calicoes in which the daughters of the house appeared, was surprising."

"I don't see the way clear to results," Judge Burnham said, perplexedly, as he and his wife walked on the piazza after breakfast and continued the discussion of ways and means. "If the Ferris tribe vacate to-day, as I have just intimated to the head of the family is extremely desirable, what are you to do for help until such time as something competent in that line can be secured, always supposing that there *is* such a thing in existence? I remember what an experience you have been having in your father's house in the line of help."

"Oh, well," said Ruth, brightly, "we had the small-pox, you know; that makes a difference. They have excellent servants there now, and, indeed, we generally have had. My housekeeping troubles did not lie in that direction. I have a plan; I don't know what you will think of it. I am afraid you will be very much surprised?"

"No, I shall not," he interrupted her to say, "I have gotten beyond the condition of surprise at anything which you may do or propose."

Then she went on with her story.

"I thought it all over last night, and if she will do it, I think I see my way clear, and I am almost sure she will, for, really, I never knew a more unselfish girl in my life."

"I dare say," her husband said, regarding her with an amused air. "Perhaps I might agree with you if you will enlighten me as to which of the patterns of domestic unselfishness you have in mind. Did she reign in your household since my knowledge of it began?"

"Oh, I am not speaking of *hired* help," Ruth said, and a vivid flush brightened her cheeks. "I was thinking of my sister. It is her help I have in mind."

"Susan!" he exclaimed, and then was suddenly silent. His face showed that, after all, she had surprised him.

There was much talk about it after that, and the discussion finally ended in their taking passage in the mail-wagon, about which Judge Burnham had spoken the day before, and jogging together to the train. There was so much to be done that Ruth had not the patience to wait until another day, besides their departure would give the Ferris family a chance to hasten *their* movements. On the way to the cars Judge Burnham mentally resolved that his first leisure moments should be spent in selecting horses and a driver, since he was to become a country gentleman. Whether he would or not, it became him to look out for conveniences.

Seated again in the train, and made comfortable by her watchful husband, Ruth took time to smile over the variety of experiences through which she had gone during the less than twenty-four hours since she sat there before. It seemed to her that she had lived a little life-time, and learned a great deal, and it seemed a wonderful thing that she was actually going to Susan Erskine with a petition for help. Who could have supposed that *she*, Ruth Erskine, would ever have reached such a period in her history that she would turn to her as the only available source of supply and comfort. A great deal of thinking can be done in one night, and Ruth had lain awake and gone over her ground with steady gaze and a determined heart. It surprised her that things had not looked plainer to her before. "Why couldn't I have seen this way, yesterday, before I left home?" she asked herself, but the wonder was that she had seen it thus early.

Very much surprised were the Erskine household to see their bride of less than twenty-four hours' standing appear while they still lingered over their breakfast-table!

"We live in the country, you know," was Ruth's composed explanation of the early advent. "Country people are up hours before town people have stirred; I always knew that."

"Land alive!" said Mrs. Judge Erskine, and then for a whole minute she was silent. She confided to Ruth, long afterward, that for about five minutes her "heart was in her mouth," for she surely thought they had quarrelled and parted!

"Though I thought at the time," she explained, "that if you *had* got sick of it a'ready you wouldn't have come back together, and have walked into the dining-room in that friendly fashion. But, then, I remembered that you never did things like anybody else in this world, and if you had made up your mind to come back home again, and leave your husband, you would be sure to pick out a way of doing it that no other mortal would ever have thought of!"

"I am going to my room," Ruth said presently. "Judge Burnham, I will hasten, and be ready to go down town with you in a very little while. Susan, will you come with me, please? I want to talk to you."

And Susan arose with alacrity, a pleasant smile lighting her plain face. There was a sound of sisterliness in the tone, which she had watched and waited for, but rarely heard.

"I have come on the strangest errand," Ruth said, dropping into her own favorite chair, as the door of her old room closed after them. "I feel as if I were at least a year older than I was yesterday. I have thought so much. First of all, Susan, I want to tell you something. I have found something. I have come close to Jesus — I mean he has come close to me. He has almost shown me himself. I don't know how to tell you about it, and indeed I am not sure that there is anything to *tell*. But it is a great deal to have experienced. I seem to have heard him say, Come to *me*. Why do you struggle and plan and toss yourself about? Haven't I promised you *rest?*" And, Susan, I do believe he spoke to my heart; why not?"

"Why not, indeed!" said Susan, "when he has repeated the message so many times. Ruth, I am *so* glad!"

Then Ruth ran rapidly from that subject to less important ones, giving her sister a picture, in brief, of the new home, closing with the sentence:

"Now I am in a dilemma. I can't keep any of the Ferris family for an hour, and I can't introduce new servants until things are in different shape, and I can't get them into different shape until I have help. Do you see what I am to do?"

"Yes," said Susan, with a bright smile, "you need a sister; one who knows how to help in all household matters, and yet who knows how to keep her tongue reasonably quiet as to what she found. I know how servants gossip, some of them. That Rosie we had for a week tried to tell me things about Mrs. Dr. Blakeman's kitchen that would make her feel like fainting if she knew it. A sister is just exactly what you need in this emergency. Will you let her step into the gap and show you how nicely she can fill it?"

"*Will* you?" Ruth asked, eagerly. "That is just exactly what I wanted to say, though I didn't like to say it, for fear you would misunderstand, not realize, you know, that it is because we don't want to go out of the *family* for assistance just now that we needed you so much."

Recognized at last in *words* as a member of the family! An unpremeditated sentence, evidently from the heart. It was what Susan Erskine had been patiently biding her time and waiting for. It had come sooner than she expected. It made her cheeks glow.

"I will go home with you at once," she said, in a business-like way. "There is nothing to hinder. The machinery of this house is in running order again. That new second girl is a treasure, Ruth, and, by the way, she has a sister who might develop into a treasure for you.

Now let me see if I understand things. What do you want to do first?"

"First," said Ruth, smiling, "I need to go shopping. It is my *forte*, you know. I like to buy things, and at last there is certainly occasion for my buying. Susan, you have no idea how much is wanted. Everything in every line is necessary, and Judge Burnham has left all to me. We need paper-hangers and painters, and all that sort of thing, but of course he will attend to those things. Our plan is to return to-night with a load of necessities. Judge Burnham is going to hire a team at once, and have it loaded. But what *are* the first necessities? Where shall I begin?"

"Begin with a pencil and paper," said Susan, seizing upon them and seating herself. "Now, let us be methodical. My teacher in mathematics once told me that I was nothing if I was not methodical. Kitchen first — no, dining-room, because we shall have to eat even before we get the house in order. What is a necessity to that table before you can have a comfortable meal?"

Then they plunged into business. Two women, thoroughly in earnest, pencil and paper in hand, bank check in pocket, organization well developed in both of them, and the need of speed apparent, can accomplish surprising things in the way of plans in an hour of time, especially when one is persistently methodical.

When Mrs. Burnham arose and drew her wrap around her preparatory to joining the husband, who was waiting below, she felt as though a week's work had been accomplished. Besides, they had been cheery together, these two — been in a different mood toward each other from what had ever appeared before. Susan was so sensible, so quick-witted, so clear-sighted as to what needed doing first, and as to ways of doing the soonest, and withal her matter-of-course way of saying " we " when she spoke of the work to arrange, made her appear such a tower of strength to Ruth, who knew so well her own delinquencies in the direction of housework, and who had thoroughly tested Susan's practical knowledge.

" Land alive ! " ejaculated Mrs. Erskine, when, after Ruth's departure, the new arrangements were presented to her for approval. " Who would have thought she would have to come after you, in less than a day after she set out to do for herself. So capable as she is, too, though I don't suppose she knows much more than a kitten about housework. How should she? Well, I'm glad I had you learn all them things. What we'd have done this winter if I hadn't is more than *I* can see through. Well, well, child, I don't know how we are going to get along without you. Your pa sets great store by you; I can see it every day; and what if I should have another turn of sick headache while you're gone! Though, for that matter, I don't believe I will. I guess going through the small-pox cured them headaches. I ain't had one since. And so she needs you right off? Well, poor thing! I don't know what she *would* do without you, I'm sure. Them girls ain't efficient, I dare say; girls never are. You learn 'em how, Susan; you can do it, if anybody can, and that'll be doing 'em a good turn."

Susan discreetly kept her own counsel about "them girls," and quietly and swiftly packed her satchel, not without an exultant song at her heart. This beautiful sister, whose love she had craved, seemed very near to her this morning.

CHAPTER XXI.

TRYING QUESTIONS.

YOU are to imagine much that was done inside that long, low house on the hill during the next three weeks. A great deal can be done in three weeks' time. What *was* actually accomplished would fill a good-sized volume; so it is well that you are to imagine instead of read about it. A great many wheels of progress were started during that very first day — Ruth among the stores, Judge Burnham among the paper-hangers, painters and draymen, Susan in the Erskine attic, sorting out and packing many things that, according to Judge Erskine's orders, were Ruth's exclusive property. By the time the five o'clock train received the three, they were tired and satisfied.

Tired though they were, it was as late as midnight before all the household settled into rest. Susan dropped into her place as naturally as though it had been waiting for her all these years. The Ferris family were departed bag and baggage, and the two Burnhams left behind were red-eyed and disconsolate. Why not? The Ferrises were the only friends they had ever known. Susan put a symyathetic arm around one and kissed the other before she had been in the house five minutes, and Ruth remembered with dismay that she had not thought of doing such a thing. And, indeed, if I must tell you the truth concerning her, it seemed almost an impossible thing to do! She had been for so many years in the habit of bestowing her kisses rarely and to such an exceedingly limited number of persons. Then they betook themselves, Susan and Seraphina, to the kitchen. Confusion reigned. So it did all over the house, except in the locked-up purity of Ruth's two rooms. But before midnight there was a comfortable place for Susan to sleep and most satisfactory preparations in line for a breakfast the next morning.

It was that next morning which gave the two Burnham girls their first touch of a cultured home. There was a little room, conveniently situated as regarded the kitchen, which the instinct of taste had made Ruth select at the first glance as a dining-room. Thither she and Susan repaired early in the evening to make a survey.

"It needs painting," said Susan, scanning the wood-work critically, "and papering; and then, with a pretty carpet, it will be just the thing. But, in the meantime, it is clean, and we can set the breakfast-table here to-morrow morning, can't we?"

"If we can get it in here to set," Ruth answered, in a dubious tone. "It is a long, horribly-shaped table, and none of *our* furniture will be here, you know."

"Oh, I see my way out of that. There is a little table in that pantry, or milk-room, or whatever is the name of it, that will do nicely for a dining-table until we get settled; and, Ruth, shall we have some of my muffins for breakfast? You remember Judge Burnham used to like them when we gave them to him occasionally for tea. Oh, girls! I can make delicious muffins, and if you are both down here by six o'clock to-morrow morning I will teach you how, the first thing I do."

This last to the two bewildered girls, who stood waiting to see what astonishing thing would happen next. As for Ruth, she went upstairs to that gem of a room, smiling over the strangeness of the thought that Susan was downstairs in their kitchen, hers and Judge Burnham's, planning with his daughters to have muffins for breakfast! Also, she thought, with a sense of satisfaction, of the great trunk packed with silver, rare old pieces of her mother's own, which had been held sacred for her during all these years, and of the smaller and newer trunk containing table drapery, which was a marvel of fineness and whiteness. Both trunks had journeyed hither several days ago, and had this night been opened to secure certain things which Susan's morning plans had called for.

So it was to the little room that the family came the next morning, with its south window,

into which the September sun slanted its rays
cheerily. The room itself was carpetless, and
the chairs were wooden, and there was no other
attempt at furniture. But the table, laid in
snowy whiteness, and the napkins large and fine
and of delicate pattern, and the silver service
gleaming before Ruth's place, and the silver
forks and solid silver spoons, and the glittering
goblets and delicate china — for Susan had actually unpacked and washed and arranged Ruth's
mother's china — to say nothing of the aroma of
coffee floating in the air, and mingling not unpleasantly with the whiff of a vase of autumn
roses which blushed before Ruth's plate.

All these things were a lesson in home refinements such as a week of talking would never
have accomplished, and which the Burnham
girls sat down to for the first time in their lives.
It was curious to notice the effect on them.
Their conspicuous calicoes and stretched-back
hair and ungainly shoes were still painfully visible. But, for the first time, apparent'y, it
dawned upon them that things didn't match.
They surveyed the table, which was as a picture
to them, and then, with instinctive movements,

essayed to hide their awkward shoes under their too short dresses, and blushed painfully over the impossibility of doing so. Ruth noticed it, and smiled. They would be ready for her hand, she fancied, when she came to an hour of leisure to arrange for them.

That breakfast scene was a cheery one. So much of home had already entered into its elements that Judge Burnham cordially pronounced Susan a fairy, and she as genially responded that she was a most substantial one, and had had two substantial helpers, with a meaning glance toward the girls.

"Indeed!" he said, in kindly tone, and then he glanced toward them.

That was a very pleasant way of showing good-will. The contrast between this breakfast and the one to which they sat down but the morning before was certainly very striking And, though the girls blushed painfully, the tone in which he had spoken, and the glance which accompanied his remark, did more for those daughters than all their father's lectures had accomplished.

Directly the muffins and the broiled steak and

the amber coffee were discussed, and, the meal concluded, business in that house commenced. Thereafter it was a scene of organized disorder. The girls, under Susan's lead, proved, notwithstanding Mrs. Judge Erskine's surmise, very "efficient" helpers. They could not enter a room properly, they could not use the King's English very well, and they knew nothing about the multitude of little accomplishments with which the girls of their age usually consume time. But it transpired that they could wash windows, and "paints," and sweep walls, and even nail carpets. They were both quick-witted and skillful over many of these employments, and the hearty laugh which occasionally rung out from their vicinity, when Susan was with them, showed plainly that they had lost their fear of her; but their embarrassment, where either their father or Ruth was concerned, did not decrease. And, indeed, in the whirl of plans which had recently come upon them, these two had little leisure to cultivate the daughters' acquaintance. Ruth, after a few attempts at helping, discreetly left the ordering of the hired helpers to Susan's skillful hands, and accompa nied her husband on daily shopping excursions, where her good taste and good sense were equally called into action.

In the course of time, and when there is a full purse to command skillful helpers, the time need not be so very long drawn out. There came a morning when it would have done your comfort-loving heart good to have walked with Judge Burnham and his wife through the reconstructed house! Nothing showy; nothing really expensive, as that term is used in the fashionable world, had been attempted. Ruth's tastes were too well cultured for that. She knew, perfectly, that what was quite in keeping with the lofty ceilings and massive windows of her father's house would be ridiculously out of place here. As you passed with her from room to room you would have realized that nothing looked out of place. Perhaps in the girl's room as much thought had been expended as in any place in that house.

Ruth had been amazed, not to say horrified, on the occasion of her first visit to their room, to find that it was carpetless, curtainless, and, I had almost said, furnitureless! An old-fash ioned, high-post bedstead, destitute of any pretense of beauty, and a plain-painted stand, holding a tin basin and a broken-nosed milk pitcher! To Ruth, whose one experience of life had to do with her father's carefully furnished house, where the servants' rooms were well supplied with the comforts, to say nothing of the luxuries of the toilet, this looked simply barbarous. Judge Burnham, too, was shocked and subdued. It had been years since he had been a caller in his daughters' room, and he had seemed to think that magic of some sort must have supplied their wants. "I furnished money whenever it was asked for," he said, regarding Ruth with a sort of appealing air. "Now, that I think of it, they were never extravagant in their demands; but I supposed I gave them enough. At least, when I thought about it at all, I assured myself that the Ferrises would certainly not be afraid to ask for more, if more was needed."

"The difficulty with the Ferris family was, that they had no tastes to expend money for," Ruth said, quietly, "but you can not wonder that the girls are not just what we would like to see them. They certainly have had no surroundings of any sort that would educate them in your direction."

After this talk he entered with heartiness into the plans for that room, and when the delicate blue and pale gold carpet was laid — and it reminded one of a sunset in a pure sky — and the white drapery was looped with blue ribbons, rural fashion, and the gold-banded china was gracefully disposed on the toilet case, and the dressing-bureau was adorned with all the little daintinesses which Ruth understood so well how to scatter, even to a blue and gold vase full of sweet-scented blossoms, and the pretty cottage bedstead was luxuriously draped in spotless white, plump pillows, ruffled pillow shams, all complete, Ruth stood back and surveyed the entire effect with the most intense satisfaction. What said the girls? Well, they *said* nothing. But their blazing cheeks and suspiciously wet eyes looked volumes, and for several days they stepped about that room in a tiptoe fashion which would have amused Ruth, had she seen it. They could not rally from the feeling that everything about them was so delicate and pure that to breathe upon, or touch, would be to mar a work of art.

Meantime, other matters had been progressing. Ruth had lain awake half of one night and studied the immortal question of dress. She had met and battled with, and conquered half a dozen forms of pride, and then had boldly announced at the next morning's breakfast-table, the following:

"Judge Burnham, the girls and I want to go to the city to attend to some dress-making. Shall we go in that mail-wagon, or how?"

Before this, I should have explained to you that Judge Burnham had been, for some days, in an active state of trying horses, examining carriages, and interviewing professional drivers. Also, several horses and carriages had waited on them for trial, so that Ruth had taken several rides to the cars on trial, and had once suggested that perhaps it would be as economical a way of keeping a carriage as any, this spending the season in making a choice. Therefore Judge Burnham laughed as he answered:

"Why, no, there is to be a trial span here in time for the ten o'clock train. I was about to propose a ride in honor of that occasion. Are you going into town for the day?"

Ruth laughed.

"For the week, I am afraid. We shall probably be detained at the dressmaker's for some time, and, after that, I have many errands to do."

Now the form in which her pride had met her last, was the shrinking from going to town, and above all, going to the fashionable dressmaking and millinery establishments with those strange-looking companions, for a critical survey of their wardrobe revealed the fact that they had nothing which she considered decent. This was not the first time that she had taken the subject into consideration. On the contrary, it had been present with her during her shopping excursions, and she had blessed the instinct which enabled her to see at a glance just what shade or tint would suit the opposite complexions of the two girls.

She had visited her dressmaker and made arrangements with her for service. But the question had been, whether she could not smuggle them off in some way to a quieter street among the less fashionable workers, and secure for them a respectable outfit in which to appear at Madame Delfort's. It was over these and kindred plans that she had lain awake, and finally abandoned them all, and resolved upon outright unconcern in regard to what others might say or think. Nevertheless she winced when the two girls came down arrayed in their best, bright plaids — for Mrs. Ferris' taste had run entirely in that direction — cheap hat adorned with cheap flowers and brilliant ribbons, both flowers and ribbons more or less soiled, and with no gloves at all. Seraphina reported that she *had lost* hers, and Araminta, that she *couldn't find hers*. Between those two states there is a distinction, though it may not appear at first sight.

The trial carriage had arrived, and Judge Burnham seated his party, himself wearing a disturbed face. He did not like the appearance of the company with which he was to go to town. Ruth had thought of this, and had tried to plan differently, but with a man's obtuseness he had *not* thought of it, and could not, or would not understand why he should go in on the ten o'clock train, and the rest wait until twelve, especially when his wife admitted herself to be in haste and they might all go together. Fairly seated opposite his daughters, he saw a reason for having gone earlier, and even looked about him, nervously, as the carriage neared the depot, wishing there was yet some chance of escape.

A way opened. "Ah, good-morning, Judge! this is fortunate. I am in search of you." This was the greeting which he received from the depot door. And he left Ruth standing on the steps and went forward to shake hands with a tall, gray-haired man, in the prime of life. He came back after a few moments, speaking rapidly. "Ruth, that is Parsons, the famous criminal lawyer; he wants to consult me in regard to a case, and is going farther on by the next train in search of a clue. I guess, after all, I shall have to wait here for the twelve o'clock, and have a talk with him; that is, if you do not object."

"Oh, not at all!" Ruth said, breathing more freely. Her husband's daughters were less of a cross to her without him than with him. Every man he met on the train knew and came to talk with him, while she was a stranger. The famous criminal lawyer moved toward them, looking interested, and Judge Burnham could hardly escape the ceremony of introduction.

"Ah!" he said, bowing low to Mrs. Burnham, "very happy to meet you, madam? I have known your husband for several years. I hear you are just getting settled at your country-seat. Terrible task, isn't it? But pays, I suppose, when one gets fairly settled. I didn't know until the other day that you were rural in your tastes, Judge Burnham?"

All these sentences, spoken in the man-of-the-world tone, which indicates that the person is talking for the sake of filling the time, and all the while his practiced eye was taking in the group — Judge Burnham with a slightly embarrassed manner and somewhat flushed face; his elegant, high-bred wife, who was a trifle pale as she was wont to be under strong feeling of any sort; and the two girls, in *outre* attire, standing a little apart, with wide eyes and flaming cheeks, staring painfully. The criminal lawyer seemed to think that the position demanded more words from him. "You are the victims of the usual American nuisance, I see," with the slightest possible inclination of his head toward the two.

"The inefficiency of hired help is really the social puzzle of this country, I think. Foreigners have immensely the advantage of us. Just returning a relay of the condemned sort I suppose?"

There was the rising inflection to his sentence which marks a question, and yet he rattled on, precisely like a man who expects no answer. Was it because the train sounded its warning-whistle just then, that Judge Burnham, though his face flushed and his eyes flashed, did not correct the criminal lawyer's mistake?

CHAPTER XXII.

"THAT WHICH SATISFIETH NOT."

FAIRLY seated in the train, Ruth Burnham gave herself up to gloominess over her own planning. The episode with the famous criminal lawyer not having served to sweeten her way, she speedily determined on making as little a cross of the rest of it as she could, too fully realizing that, plan as she would, the way was a *cross*. She still shrank from the fashionable "Madame's," and her fashionable corps of workers. Perhaps the worriment was what she deserved for being so fashionable in her desires that she could not bring herself to look up an obscure back street with a modest sign, and thus help along the large army of workers, who can not be fashionable — though really, there are two sides to even that question. She understood that as a rule, the work done from that back street would be a continual source of mortification to her — a constant strain on her temper, so long as the garments lasted. After all, it is not so much the desire to be in the height of the fashion that sends women to the extravagantly high-priced *modistes*, as a knowledge of the fact that as a rule, the low-priced ones do not understand their business, and will succeed in making a bungle of any work which they undertake. When there shall arise a class of women who have carefully learned how to cut and make ordinary garments, in the best manner, the cry of hard times, among such workers, will be less frequently heard.

Ruth concluded not to risk contact with chance acquaintances in street-cars; but, directly she reached the city, took a carriage to a store where she was a stranger, and did some rapid transforming work. Two stylish wraps, selected with due reference to their qualifications for covering much objectionable toilet underneath —

selected, too, with careful reference to the height and shape and complexion of the wearers ; then gloves that were strong and neat-fitting and shapely; then hats of easily-donned stamp, gracefully, yet slightly trimmed; and, really, Judge Burnham would hardly have recognized his daughters. Ruth surveyed them with satisfaction ; and, if they could have been fitted at the " Madame's," without removing those stylish mantles, she would have drawn a sigh of relief. As it was, she still had that to dread, and a real ordeal it was. Those who condemn her for exhibiting much false pride and foolish lack of independence have probably never been tried in the same way. You have, of course, observed that people's own peculiar trials are the ones for which they have sympathy. They are harder, too, to bear, than any other person's.

Ruth was not one whit behind the multitude, in her way of thinking about herself. As she stood in the " Madame's " apartments and endured the well-bred stares and the well-bred impudence — for there really is such a thing as what might be called well-bred impudence — she set her teeth hard, and ruled that the color *should not* rush into her face, and, also, that the "Madame" should have no more of her custom, from this time forth And yet, when she came to cooler moments, she tried to reason within herself, as to how the woman was to blame. What had she said, or looked, that was not, under the circumstances, most natural?

All these questions Ruth held, for the time being, at bay, and arranged and directed and criticised with her usual calm superiority of manner, and with the assurance of one who knew exactly what she wanted, and intended not to stop short of entire satisfaction. And she didn't. She was more critical and troublesome, even, than usual; and the "Madame" would have told you that that was unnecessary. And, at last, after many delays, and changes of plan and trimmings, and changes of patterns, involving vexatious delays on "Madame's" part, they were free of her for the day, and could pursue their round of shopping more at leisure. But Ruth was in no mood for shopping, other than the necessary things that must be ordered to the "Madame's" without delay. She was tired and fretted; she wanted something to cool and quiet her.

She dispatched the necessary shopping with great care, indeed, but with unusual speed, leaving the girls, meantime, seated in the carriage, instead of in the great store, where they would have delighted to be.

The business of lunching had been dispatched some time before — as soon, indeed, as they had left the dress-making establishment. Ruth had chosen an obscure place for refreshment, not choosing to risk the danger of fashionable acquaintances, at the places with which she was familiar. Consequently, she had been able to do little else than gather her skirts about her, to protect them from careless and hurried waiters, and to curl her aristocratic nose behind her handkerchief, at the unwonted smells combining around her; while the girls, famished by the drain on their nerves, and having, by reason of the excitement of the morning, been unable to indulge in much breakfast, made a hearty meal, not at all disturbed by the sights and sounds and odors which made eating an impossibility to Ruth. This little matter served to add to her discomfort and her sense of gloom; for, when people are hungry, they are much more ready to yield to gloom. All the shopping done that she could bring herself to give attention to, she consulted her watch, and learned with dismay, that there was an hour and a half before train-time. What was to be done with it?

She thought of her husband's office; but suppose the criminal lawyer should be there? In any case, there would be those dreadful students to stare, and nudge each other and giggle. Ruth dreaded a giggle more than she did a bullet. Assuredly, she would not go there! Neither was her city home to be thought of. She was not in a mood to present her husband's daughters to Mrs. Judge Erskine; neither did she intend that those daughters, in their present attire, or with their present attainments, should come in contact with her. So, as the gloomy-faced woman rode listlessly along, on an up-town car, while the two girls were bobbing their heads swiftly from one window to another, endeavoring to take in all the strange sights, she was engaged in trying to decide what to do with time. A blackboard bulletin, before one of the public halls, caught her notice, and her quick eye took in the large lettering: "*Bible Reading! Harry Morehouse! Here, at Four O'clock! Come!*" Before she had reached the inviting word, she had signaled the car, and the bewildered girls were following her whither she would.

"There is an hour or more before we can go home," she said in explanation. "Let us go to this meeting. Perhaps it will be interesting."

They were entirely willing; in fact, they were in a state of maze. Anything that this remarkable woman — who knew her way so composedly through this great whirling city — suggested, they were willing to help carry out. So they mounted the steps to the large, light, social-looking room, where people were already thronging in. No acquaintances to be feared here. Ruth did not now know many who frequented such meetings, or were to be found in this part of the city. In the distance she caught a glimpse of Marion, but she shrank back, unwilling to be recognized even by her; for Marion had her beautiful daughter beside her, and the contrast would be too strikingly painful. Presently the meeting opened. Ruth looked about her for

Harry Morehouse, a name with which she was not unfamiliar. But she almost curled her lip in disappointment, she was so amazed at the insignificance of this little, boyish man! "As if *he* could help anybody!" her heart said, in scorn. "What exaggerated reports do get into the papers about people!" And then, presently, she did just what many another person has done, who has listened to Harry Morehouse's rendering of Scripture — forgot to think of the man, and gave earnest heed to the words which he was reading; words which, someway, had a sound — strangely familiar though they were — as if she had never heard them before.

"Wherefore do ye spend money for that which is not bread? and your labor for that which satisfieth not? Hearken diligently unto me, and eat ye that which is good, and let your soul delight itself in fatness." What was there in the familiar verse that thrilled so through Ruth Burnham's soul? "That which satisfieth not." She needed only her own experience to show her that one who understood the human heart spoke those words! How freely she had been giving labor! and how strangely unsatisfy ing it all seemed to her to-day! She fairly hungered and thirsted after a higher grasp of the Infinite Arm, reached down. A great longing came over her to hide herself away in him. She was so tired and so tried, and a long line of petty trials stared her in the face. She felt like turning away from them all; and yet she mustn't. Well, then, she felt like reaching higher ground — getting up where the air was purer — where these endless details of dress and position would trouble her less — where such women as "Madame," the dressmaker, would have no power to flush her cheek and set her heart to angry beatings by a high-bred stare. Suddenly a new thought flashed across her heart. These girls—what had she been doing for them? How had she been trying to satisfy them? In the days that they had spent together, she remembered that she had not once alluded, even in the most remote manner, to anything higher, or better, or more satisfying, than these new things, which, at best, were to perish with the using. Had she not, by her example, left the impress of her first influence upon them to the effect that well-furnished rooms and carefully-adorned bodies were *the* important things on which to spend one's strength?

"Well," she said within her disturbed self, "I have no time."

"No time?" inquired that other inner self, which is forever at war with its fellow. "Is it because you have been employed on *more* important matters?"

This almost angered Ruth; it flushed her face, and she said:

"There is a proper time for all things."

"Yes," said the other one, "and is the proper time to attend to this most important concern with which we have to do in life *after* all the lesser matters are disposed of?"

Then Ruth roused, and gave her heart some searching into. Was it possible that she had really been teaching those girls that she considered the matter of their outward adorning more important than anything else connected with them! If actions speak even louder than words, and if she had acted the one, and not so much as *spoken about* the other, what else could they think?

"I am glad," she told herself, "that I brough'

them into this meeting. At least they will get a different idea here."

Then she turned and looked at them. *Would* they get different ideas, or had the first taken root, leaving at least no *present* room for other growths?

Miss Seraphina was spreading her hand carefully out on her lap, and contemplating with eyes of unmistakable admiration the color and texture and fit of her new gloves! It was altogether probable that she had never worn well-fitting gloves before, and she felt their importance. The other sister was evidently as totally absorbed in the trimness of her neatly-fitting kid boot, the advent of which had made her foot a stranger to herself, with which she was trying to get acquainted, as though Harry Morehouse and his wonderful new Bible had been in London at that moment! A strange pang thrilled the heart of the woman who was trying in her youth to be a mother to these two, as she looked at their absorbed faces and followed the direction of their eyes. Was that simply the necessary result of new refinements? Would these all sink into their proper and subordinate places directly the newness and strangeness had worn off, or was this really a wave of her own influence which was going to increase in power as surely as it was fed?

Now, this thought did not rest her; and while it was desirable in itself that she should be thus early roused to the sense of danger there might be in flooding these young creatures with this world's vanities, that wise old enemy, Satan, was on the alert to make the whole matter into thorns with which to prick Ruth's tired heart, and in obliging her thoughts to revolve around this center, never widening it nor seeing her way out of the maze, yet effectually shutting her off from the practical help which awaited her through the channel of Harry Morehouse's Bible.

Somebody has said that, whoever else stays away from a religious meeting, Satan never does. Was there ever a truer statement? If he would only appear in his natural character, instead of, as in this instance, transforming himself into a goad, and pressing hard against the nerves that were already strained to their utmost!

On the whole, Mrs. Judge Burnham went

home on the five o'clock train thoroughly wearied in body and mind, and with a haunting sense of disappointment pressing down her spirits. She had accomplished that which she had in the morning started to do. She had been successful in all her undertakings, and could feel that things were now in train for making transformation in the outward appearance of these hitherto neglected girls. A laudable undertaking, certainly, so it was held in its place, but she could not get her heart away from the sentence: **" And your labor for that which satisfieth not."**

CHAPTER XXIII.

WHEREFORE?

NOW, I am afraid you will laugh over the matter which appeared next to Ruth Burnham in the shape of a trial. Yet, if you have not lived long enough in this world to be in sympathy with the *little* trials, which, in certain states of mind, look large, either your experience is not extensive or your *sympathies* not large. It was no greater matter than the hair which belonged to Judge Burnham's daughters. But really if you *could* have seen the trying way in which they managed to disfigure their heads with this part of their adorning, you would have felt that some action was demanded

Ruth knew exactly how each head ought to be dressed; she could almost see the effect that would be produced by a skillful and easily attainable arrangement. Then where the trial? Why, perhaps, if you are not made up of that cruelly sensitive type of women — and I am sure I hope you are not — it will be difficult to make plain to you how Ruth shrank from touching that hair! Human hair, other than her own was a thing which she desired to keep at a respectful distance. She could admire it, when well cared for, and she did most heartily. But to *care* for it, to comb and brush and fondle over *any* person's hair, was to Ruth, or would have been had she ever been called upon to suffer in that line, a positive martyrdom. Now add to this the fact that this shrinking from the work increased tenfold when it had to do with any person who was not *very* dear and precious, and possibly you can comprehend why she wore so troubled a face that Saturday evening, and gazed at those hopeless heads opposite her, and wondered how a transformation was to be brought about. She was hopeless as regarded teaching the intricacies of any becoming twist or curl. In time, with

patience and with often taking hold and obliging
the refractory hairs to lie in their place, it might
be accomplished; and here poor Ruth shivered
over the horrors of a possible future experience.
But to get them ready to appear at church the
next morning, without a personal encounter,
was not to be hoped for

This Saturday evening, although the family
had been three weeks in their new home, was
the first in which they were planning for church.
The little church in the village had been closed
for a longer space of time than that, undergoing
repairs, and the first Sabbath after their marriage Ruth had contrived to plan and work herself into an exhaustive headache that had to be
succumbed to and petted all day. The next
they had been forced to spend in the city, by
reason of having missed the last train out on
Saturday. Now here they were on the eve of
the third, and Ruth at least had been planning
toward the little stone church around the corner.
Everything was in readiness. The new dresses
and the new bonnets and the new gloves, and
all the new and bewildering paraphernalia of
the toilet had arrived from the city, the last

package only the evening before, and but for that dreadful hair Ruth would have been happy over the thought of the effect to be produced by the next morning's toilet.

It was Susan who at last, and in an unexpected manner, came to the rescue, just as she had stepped in and rescued Ruth from a hundred trials, both seen and unseen, during the experiences of the last three weeks. She did her part so naturally, too, as one who simply happened along at the right moment, without having understood any special need for it. Perhaps there is no rarer or more perfect way of bearing one another's burdens than this apparently unconscious one.

They sat in the cheery sitting-room — Ruth would not have it called a parlor — and in no part of the house had the transformation been more complete than in that square, rag-carpeted, paper-curtained, and unhome-like room. Judge Burnham was reading certain business letters that seemed to perplex him. The girls were wishing that they could invent some excuse for escaping early from the room to their own, that they might have another look at all the beauties of their wardrobe, and Ruth was gazing at them with a distressed air and manner, and thinking of hair! Susan, glancing up from her glove-mending, followed the direction of Ruth's eyes for a moment, then she spoke her thoughts.

"I just *long* to get hold of your hair."

The remark seemed to be addressed to the two girls, and was so in keeping with Ruth's thoughts that she started and flushed, wondering for an instant whether it were possible for Susan to know what they were. The girls laughed, and looked pleased at her interest.

"Your hair would curl beautifully," Susan added, addressing the elder sister. "And those wide braids in which heavy hair is arranged now would just fit Minta's face. Don't you think so, Ruth?"

"Yes," said Ruth, promptly, "I am sure of it. But I don't know that she could get them looped right."

"Oh yes, she could. It is very easy after one knows how. Girls, I am an excellent barber. Suppose we go up-stairs and try my skill? I can show you so that you can arrange that part of your toilet in the morning in less time than it usually takes."

This plan was immediately carried out, the three going up-stairs with merry voices, Susan's cheery one being heard to say:

"Oh, you don't understand half my accomplishments yet; there are ever so many things I can do."

"That is a fact," said Judge Burnham, with emphasis. "She is a very treasure in the house. I used to pity you, Ruth, but, upon my word, so far as she is concerned, I am not sure that there was any room for pity."

"There was not," Ruth said, heartily. "It took me a long time to realize it, but she has been from the first day of her coming to our home a blessing to me."

And so strange are these hearts of ours, touched oftentimes by words or deeds apparently so slight, Ruth felt the little episode of the hair-dressing as something that called forth very tender feeling for her sister. She began to have a dim idea of what a blessing might be hidden in a simple, quiet life, constantly unselfish in so-called *little* things.

So it came to pass that, on a lovely Sabbath morning, the Burnham family were one and all making ready to appear as a family in the little stone church. The girls had been there, more or less, on Sabbaths, during their lives. Years ago Judge Burnham used to go occasionally, when he felt like it. But it had been many a year since he had been seen inside the unpretending little building. Ruth, of course, had never been, and the circumstances surrounding them all were so new and strange that it was almost like a company of strangers being introduced into home-life together.

The two girls came down a trifle earlier than the others, and were in the hall near the doorway, where the soft, yellow sunlight rested on them, when Judge Burnham descended the stairs. Half-way down he paused, with a surprised, irresolute air, as his eyes rested on the two apparent strangers, and then, as one of them turned suddenly, and he caught a glimpse of her face, the surprise deepened into bewilderment. Who *were* these young ladies who were so at home in his house in the privacy of a Sabbath morning? This was the first thought.

And the second, "It is not — can it be *possible* that they are my daughters!" Then, it is almost surprising that he did not at once feel humiliated over the fact that outward adornings had power so to transform!

It was certainly a transformation! Rich, quiet-toned silks, just the right tint to accord well with skin and eyes, made in that indescribable manner which marks the finished workman, to those eyes skilled in translating it, and to other eyes it simply says, "The effect is perfect." Wraps, and hats, and gloves, and handkerchiefs — everything in keeping. And, in place of the stretched-back hair, were soft, smooth, rolling auburn curls, completely changing the expression of the wearer's face. Also, that unbecoming mass of shortish hair which had hung in such untidy uncouthness, was gone, and in its place wide, smooth braids, tastefully looped here and there with knots of ribbon of just the right shade.

Ruth should have been there at that moment to see the two, and to see Judge Burnham as he looked at them. She would have felt rewarded for her work. It certainly *was* strange what a different manner the hitherto awkward girls now assumed. A sense of conscious becomingness, if it were nothing more, had fallen upon them, and in the effort to do justice to their new selves they almost unconsciously drew the stooping shoulders straight and stood with heads erect.

"Well, upon my word!" said Judge Burnham, recovering himself at last, and advancing toward them, "I didn't know you. I wondered what strange ladies we had here. Your fall suits are certainly very becoming."

He chose to ignore the fact that fall suits were new experiences to them. Perhaps he really did not yet understand to what a new world they had been introduced. The two laughed, not unpleasantly, and the flush on their cheeks, toned, as it was, by the billows of soft ruchings about the throat, was certainly not unbecoming. They had taken long looks at themselves in their mirror, that morning, and it was not unpleasant to them to think that their father did not recognize them. They had already reached the place where they had no desire to have their past recognized. Some seed takes root promptly and grows rapidly.

You may imagine that the entrance of the Burnham party to the little stone church was an event in the eyes of the congregation. They had known the Burnham girls all their lives; but these "young ladies" they never saw before. It would have been curious to a student of human nature to have studied the effect which their changed appearance made on the different characters present. Certain ones looked unaffected and unconcealed amazement; others gazed up at them, and returned their nods of recognition with respectful bows, seeming to look upon them as people who had moved to an immense distance from themselves; and there were those who resented the removal, and tossed their heads and said, with their eyes, and the shape of their mouths, that they "considered themselves quite as good as those Burnham girls, if they were all decked out like peacocks!"

As for Judge Burnham, the shade of satisfied pride, in place of the mortification which he had schooled himself to feel, repaid his wife for her three weeks of effort.

Then she tried to turn away from the question of personal appearance, and give herself to the service; but she was both surprised and pained to find that, in her well-meant efforts to place these girls in their proper position before others, she had, someway, lost ground spiritually. It was all very well to resolve to turn her thoughts away from the girls, and their dresses, and their bonnets, and their hair, and their manners, but it was another thing to accomplish it. She found what, possibly, we have each discovered by experience, that it was not easy to get away on Sabbath, in church, from that which had absorbed us during the week, and indeed, a fair share of the early Sabbath itself. Try as she would to join in hymn, or Bible-reading, or even prayers, she found her mind wandering to such trivial questions as whether, after all, a shade lighter of the silk would have fitted Minta's peculiar complexion better, or whether those gloves were not a trifle large. These thoughts were very hateful to her. She struggled hard to get away from them, and was amazed and distressed beyond measure to find that they held her captive. She waited eagerly for the sermon, hoping that it would be such an one as would hold her attention for her, since she was not able to control it herself; and behold, the text announced was one which, indeed, helped her wandering thoughts, but threw her back into the very midst of the gloom which had pressed her heart the last time she heard those words: "Wherefore do ye spend money for that which is not bread? and your labor for that which satisfieth not?" Again her answering conscience said that was what she had been doing. Money and time and strength freely given for that which was not bread!

It had not fed her soul; on the contrary, it, or something else, had starved her. Well, what was the trouble? She had surely done that which was her duty? Yes, but did a revealing spirit whisper the words in her ear, just then?—"These ought ye to have done, and not to have left the other undone." She had been *absorbed* in her labor; she had put these things first. She had risen and gone about the day, too hurried for other than a word of prayer—too hurried for any private reading. She had retired at night, too wearied in mind and body for any prayer at all! She was starved! much time gone, and no bread for her hungry soul! Also, having not fed herself, how could she have been expected to feed others? Even yet she had said almost nothing, to these daughters of hers, about the all-important matter. She had talked with them, often and long. All the details of the toilet had been gone over carefully, exhaustively, and she and they, and Judge Burnham himself, were satisfied with the results of her words in that direction. What about the direction which "*satisfieth?*"

How was Ruth to get away from her heart?

No, I must do her justice; that was not her cry. She did not want to get away from the awakening voice. She was distressed, she was humiliated, she was unhappy; but she wanted to find rest only through the love and patience of Jesus. She felt like a sheep who had wandered outside, even while doing work that she surely thought was set for her — as, indeed, it was; but her eyes were just opening to the fact that one can do work that the Master has set, so vigorously as to forget the resting-places which he has marked for the soul to pause and commune with him, and gather strength. She had been *working*, but not *resting*. And then, again, it was most painfully true that, because of her lack of spiritual strength, she had done but half her work. The important human side she had held to its important place, and worked faithfully for it. But the forever-more important spiritual side she had allowed to sink almost out of sight of her vision; and even, when roused by His Spirit, as He had spoken to her through that very verse, but a little time before, she had allowed her roused heart to slip back and absorb itself in the cares of this world and the adornments of fleshly bodies, while the souls waited.

Truth to tell, Ruth was not troubled any more that morning, by wandering thoughts; neither did she hear much of the earnest sermon which was preached; but, if the preacher had but known how the Holy Spirit took his text and preached to one soul for him, he would have gone home to his closet, on his knees, and thanked God for using his lips that day, in reading to that soul that questioning word.

CHAPTER XXIV.

"HEARKEN UNTO ME."

"IT passes my comprehension how a man with no more development of brain-power than that one possesses made the mistake of thinking he was called to preach!"

This was what Judge Burnham said, as he walked with his wife home from the morning service.

"Did you ever hear an effort more devoid of ideas? What possible good can he think he has accomplished, if that is his motive? Or how can he have sufficient vanity to imagine that it is other than a bore to listen to him?"

Ruth hesitated for her answer. It was not

that she had been so impressed with the sermon, it was rather the text that had been preached to her; and she did not feel personally sensitive in regard to Judge Burnham's opinion of this particular minister. I think the reason that the words struck sharply on her heart was because they revealed her husband's utter lack of sympathy with the subject matter of the sermon. He was speaking solely from a critical, intellectual standpoint, without, apparently, a conception of any spiritual power connected with the "foolishness of preaching." The sentence revealed to Ruth, as with a flash of light — such as reveals darkness — the fact that her husband had no sympathy with Christ or his servants, as such. Of course, she had known this before; but to know a thing and to *feel* it are two very different matters.

"I was not thinking of the *newness* of the truth," she said, after a little, speaking hesitatingly. "It impressed me, however. A thing does not need to be new in order to be helpful; it may be as old as the earth, and we never have given it attention."

"Possibly," he said lightly. "There are

things so old and so tiresome that we do not care to give them special attention; I am entirely willing to class that sermon among such, if you say so. I declare I had not realized that a sermon could be such a trial to me. I don't quite see what is to be done; I suppose your orthodoxy will not permit of your staying at home on Sabbath, and I'm sure we can not tolerate that sort of preaching — I suppose he calls it preaching. How shall we manage?"

Still Ruth had no answer ready. Every word that he spoke served to increase the heavy weight at her heart; and, despite her shivering effort to get away from it, there rang the question, "How can two walk together except they be agreed?" Yet she realized only too well that the time for settling that question was long past; that she had taken solemn and irrevocable vows upon her, and must abide by them. The question now was, How was she so to walk with him as not to dishonor Christ?

"I have no fault to find with the man's preaching," she said, coldly; and her husband laughed good-naturedly, and told her he appreciated her well-meant efforts to make the best of everything, but, unfortunately, she had too much brain to allow him for a moment to believe that such weak attempts at oratory satisfied her. Then he changed the subject, talking of matters as foreign to Ruth's thoughts as possible, and yet serving, by their very distance from her heart, to press the weight of pain deeper. Her eyes once widely opened, it seemed that everything which occured that day served to show her more plainly the gulf which lay between her ideas, and plans, and hopes, and those of her husband.

"What a glorious day this is!" he had said, as they turned from the dinner table. "I declare I believe the country *is* ahead of the city! on such days as these, any way. Ruth, what do you say to a ride? It would be a good time to explore that winding road which seemed to stretch away into nowhere."

While he waited, he watched with surprise the flush which deepened and spread on his wife's face. It so happened that the question of Sabbath riding for pleasure was one which had come up incidentally for discussion one evening at Flossy Shipley's, during Mr. Roberts' visit, and

Ruth, who had taken the popular view of innocent Sabbath recreation, had discussed the matter with keen relish, finding Mr. Roberts able to meet her at every point. She had been first annoyed to find her position open to so much objection, then interested to study the question in all its bearings, and ended, as such a frank, intelligent and thoroughly sincere nature as her's must end, in abandoning a position which she saw was untenable, and coming strongly over to the other side; since which time the observance of the Sabbath had been one of her strong points. Judge Burnham had respected her scruples, so far as he knew them, but, truth to tell, he did not understand them very well. Having no personal principle in the matter by which to judge, he was in danger of erring in unthought of directions, and every new phase of the same question demanded a new line of reasoning. It had not so much as occurred to him that his wife would see any impropriety in riding out in her own carriage, on the Sabbath day, with her husband, on a quiet, unfrequented country road.

While she hesitated he watched her curiously.

"Well," he said, laughing, at last, "what is

the trouble? You look as though I had broken all the commands in the Decalogue. Am I on forbidden ground now?"

"Not *all* the commands," Ruth said, trying to smile; "but you seem to have forgotten the Fourth."

"I am not sure that I know it. I am not thoroughly posted as to the commandments — the position in which they stand at least. What is wrong, Ruth?"

"Judge Burnham, I don't like to ride out for pleasure on Sabbath."

"What! not with me? Is it wicked to have a pleasant time on Sabbath? I didn't know that. I fail to see why we can't be as good sitting together in the carriage as we are sitting together in the parlor. Or should we spend this day apart, enjoying the luxury of melancholy reflection?"

"I think you know what I mean. You are much too well versed in argument to be entirely ignorant of people's views in regard to this day."

"Upon my word, Ruth, I was never more innocent. I might be able to see some force in a young lady's objection to riding out with a young gentleman, especially in a city, or in a crowded thoroughfare, though even such things may be carried to excess; but when it comes to one's husband, and a country road where we shall not meet three people in an hour, I confess I am befogged. Susan, do you see the bearings of this case?"

"Why, I see a good many bearings which you would not admit, and possibly you could bring to bear a good many arguments which *I* would not admit. We start from different standpoints. It all resolves itself into whether we believe the word of God or not, and *I* accept it as our rule of life."

"Why, no, it doesn't. I believe the word of God; in a measure at least. I have respect for the Sabbath as an institution, and believe in its sacredness. I have no sort of fault to find with 'Remember the Sabbath day, to keep it holy.' I believe it was a good, sensible law. But we should very likely quarrel over the word 'holy.' I should object to the narrowness which made it so falsely holy that I could not enjoy a ride with my wife after church, and I should have serious doubts as to whether you could prove your side of the question from the Bible."

"Listen to one Bible argument, then," Susan said, quietly, "and tell me what you think it means. 'If thou turn away thy foot from doing thy pleasure on my holy day, and call the Sabbath a delight, the holy of the Lord, honorable, and shalt honor Him, not doing thine own ways, nor finding thine own pleasure, nor speaking thine own words.' What do you think of that argument for my side, Judge Burnham?"

The gentleman addressed looked his embarrassment and annoyance. The verse quoted sounded strangely new and solemn to him. His inner consciousness was made certain that he was not ready to gauge his Sabbath employments by that rule.

"Oh, well," he said, restlessly, "that verse would have to affect other things besides riding out in the country; it has to do with home-life, and words, and acts, as well."

"It certainly has," Susan answered. And she spoke as if she thought it in no degree lessened the force of the argument, because the obligation reached in many directions.

"I suppose," Ruth said, "there is no question but that the Sabbath is very poorly observed; still that is hardly an argument for increasing the ways for dishonoring it, is it?"

Then Judge Burnham turned on his heel and went off to the piazza, deigning no reply to the general question that his wife had put. As for herself, she struggled with the sense of pain that kept increasing, and wondered how she should shape her life. Apparently, Judge Burnham became ashamed of his rudeness, for he returned presently to the parlor, whither Ruth had gone to wait for him, and seating himself near her, with some pleasant remark as far removed from the recent subject as he could make it, took up a book and seemed to lose himself in it. Ruth followed his example, the book she took being the elegantly bound Bible that her father had sent to grace the table. Instinctively she turned to the chapter from which the haunting verse came, and slowly, carefully, read it over. Presently what had been a pretense with Judge Burnham became reality. He was interested in his book, which interest he evidenced by a burst of laughter.

"This is really rich," he said. "Listen to this sarcasm, Ruth; see if you ever heard anything touch deeper." And then he read from the sparkling, satirical, popular writer, a dozen sentences of brilliant sarcasm concerning one of the scientific questions of the day — keen, sharp, sparkling with wit and strength, but having to do with a subject for which Ruth had no sympathy at any time, and which especially jarred upon her this Sabbath afternoon. Her husband looked up from his reading to meet the answering flash of the eyes which he liked so well to see kindle, and met the objection on her face, and felt the lack of sympathy with his enjoyment. "I beg your pardon," he said, abruptly, "I had forgotten your Puritan ideas. Possibly I am infringing again on the sacredness of your Sabbath."

"I certainly think that the sentiments of that book are not in accordance with the Bible idea of the sacredness of the day." If Ruth could only have kept her voice from sounding as cold as an iceberg, she might have had some influence.

As it was, he arose with a decided frown on

his fine face. "I see, Ruth," he said, speaking as coldly as she had herself, "that we assuredly have nothing in common for this day of the week, whatever may be said of us on other days. It is a pity that the 'sacredness of the Sabbath' should be the only element of discord between husband and wife. As I am in continual danger of erring unconsciously, I will have the grace to leave you in solitude and religious enjoyment," and with a courtly bow he left her to herself, and her large, open Bible, and her sad heart.

A little later Susan came in, and stopping beside her looked down the page of the Bible. Ruth laid her finger on the words of the morning text: "It is all true, Susan," she said gravely. "I don't believe there is any person living who realizes it more fully than I do. 'That which satisfieth not.' One may do one's best, and succeed in accomplishing, and it is unsatisfying."

"Have you answered the question, Ruth, dear?"

"Whose question?"

"The Holy Spirit's — Wherefore, do ye?

That is what he asks. Do you understand why we try to satisfy our souls on husks, instead of wheat?"

"Well," Ruth said, thoughtfully, "things have to be done."

"Of course; but why should we stop among the *things* expecting satisfaction, or allow them to take other than the subordinate place they were meant to occupy? Ruth, I think the trouble with you is, you do not read the whole verse. You feel that you have proved the truth of the first part of it, in your own experience Why don't you try the rest?"

"Just what do you mean?"

"Why, listen; 'Hearken unto me, and eat ye that which is good, and let your soul delight itself in fatness.' Don't you see what an assurance that is, that the feast is spread? There is prepared that which will satisfy; why not hearken to the voice of the Master of the feast?"

Ruth lifted to her sister's face earnest eyes, that filled with tears.

"I *have* tried to 'hearken,'" she said, in a voice that was husky with feeling. "I have heard his voice and have tried to follow him and, at times, as I have told you before, he has seemed very near, but the feeling does not stay. I am up on the Mount one day, more than satisfied, and the next day I have dropped down and lost my comfort."

"Yes, I know that story in all its details. I have lived it. In my own case it was because I ceased 'hearkening' for his voice. I placed other things first. I thought first of what *I* was going to do, or have, or be, instead of putting Christ first."

"Ruth, don't you know He says: 'For I the Lord thy God am a *jealous God?*' How often I have thought of that! He *will not abide* with a divided heart; he must be *first*; and, for myself, I did not for years keep him first. God was not in *all* my thoughts."

"I don't know," Ruth said, speaking slowly after a long silence, and she spoke with a long drawn sigh.

"I don't know that I can ever get back to where I was, even three weeks ago. Something has dropped like a pall upon my joy in religion. I never had much joy in anything. Really, it isn't my nature to be joyful. Perhaps I should not expect it."

Susan, smiling, shook her head. "That won't do, you know. Joy is one of the fruits that you are commanded to bear. It is not optional with you. 'The fruit of the Spirit is love' — *joy* — you remember. It is not the joy of nature that you and I are to look for, but the joy of grace. Ruth, if I were you, I would not try to go back to three weeks ago, I would try to go back to Christ and ask him to hold you, and lead you, and speak for you, and in this, your time of special need, not to let you drop for one moment away from him."

But who shall account for the perversity of the human heart? Something in the simple, earnest words were translated by Satan to mean to Ruth a reflection against her husband. She lifted her head haughtily and the tremor went out of her voice. "I don't know what you mean by my 'time of special need;' I do not know that one's life, humanly speaking, could be more carefully shielded than mine. I have no anxiety as to Judge Burnham's position in regard to these questions; he will respect my wishes and follow my plans."

To this Susan had no answer. Had she spoken at all, she feared she would have shown Ruth that her own words were not strictly true. She believed her at this moment to be weighed down with a sense of her husband's influence over her.

When the bell tolled for evening service, Susan and the two daughters of the house came down attired for church.

"Going again?" queried Judge Burnham, with uplifted eyebrows. "Ruth and I have had enough for to-day." And Ruth, sitting back in the easy chair, with a footstool at her feet, and a sofa pillow at her head, and a volume of sacred poems in her hand, neither raised her eyes nor spoke.

"Thou shalt have no other gods before me." This sentence stayed persistently with Susan Erskine. What had it to do with Judge Burnham and his wife that they, too, should remind her of it?

CHAPTER XXV.

"BITTER – SWEET.'

A QUESTION which began to press heavily on Ruth's mind as the days went by was: What should she do when Susan went home?

It began to be apparent that all the details connected with the reconstructed house were completed; and also, that a skillful set of hired helpers were in their places. But it was equally apparent to her heart that she shrank from the thought of seeing Susan pack her trunk and go back to the Erskine homestead; she fitted so perfectly into the family life; she had already acquired such a remarkable degree of influence over the girls. They copied her ways and her words, and it had some time ago become apparent to Ruth that this sister of hers was in every respect worthy of being copied. Even her dress — taking its hints from Flossy Shipley's sweetly-spoken words, about which Ruth knew nothing — had taken such quietness of tone that, if it was not marked for its beauty, had perhaps higher praise in that it was not noticed at all, but had sunken into the minor place it was expected to fill. Ruth, in thinking the past all over, was amazed at the wholesale way in which she had finally adopted her sister. Just *when* she began to like her, so well that it was a pleasure to have her company and a trial to think of her absence, she did not know. It seemed to her now as though she had always felt so; and yet she knew that somewhere along the line of her life there must have been a decided change of feeling.

"She is just splendid, anyway!" This was the final verdict. "I don't care when I began to know it; I know it now. I wish I could have her with me always. If she and father could live out here with us, how nice it would be! Father would like the country; it would rest and strengthen him. But, oh! *that woman!*" Which two words, spoken with an intensity of emphasis that she allowed only the four walls of her room to hear, always referred to Mrs. Judge Erskine. She was quite as much of a trial as ever. Ruth could not conceive of a possibility of there ever being a time when she should want to see *her*. So she studied over the problem of how to keep Susan, and, like many another student, found, after a few days, that it was worked out for her, in a way that she would not have chosen.

The news burst like a bomb-shell into their midst, without note or warning. Judge Erskine had lost his fortune! Large though it had been, it slipped out of his grasp almost in an hour.

"The trouble has to do with small-pox and religion!" Judge Burnham said, with something very like a sneer on his handsome face. "I don't know which development should be blamed the most. During his exile from the office his clerks made some very foolish moves, as regarded investments, etc. And, then, the other disease reached such a form that he was beguiled into putting his name to two or three pieces of paper for others, on the score of friendship — a piece of idiocy that during all his sane years he had warned me, and every other business man who came to him for advice, from being beguiled into; and the result is, financial ruin."

"There are worse ruins than that!" Ruth said it haughtily; her husband's criticism of her father jarred.

"Oh, that is true enough. There are dishonorable ruins; this one is the soul of honor, and of philanthropy, for that matter. He has *so* much to sustain him, but he can't live on it. And, Ruth, if you had ever known what it was to live on nothing, you could sympathize better with that sort of ruin. The hard part for me to bear would be that it is all so unnecessary; if he had but lived up to the wisdom and business keenness which characterized all the earlier years of his life! He has taken to giving some very strange advice to his clients since he subscribed to his new views — advice which has taken thousands of dollars out of his business. 'Had to do it,' he told me; his 'conscience wouldn't allow him to do otherwise.' If that is true, I am really afraid that I couldn't afford to have a conscience; it is too expensive an article."

How much of this was sincere, and how much was a sort of sarcastic pleasantry? Ruth wished she knew. It was a new and rather startling thought that possibly the money which sustained her now had to do with the fact that her husband couldn't afford a sensitive conscience!

She put the thought away, as far from her as possible. At least, she could do nothing with it now; the time for it was past. She tried not to think what ground she had for expecting a high type of conscience from one who lived in cool dishonor of the claims of the Lord Jesus Christ.

The immediate questions were: What would her father do? Also, what was there that she could do for him?

"Oh, he will give everything up," Judge Burnham said; "every penny; house, and landed property, and household goods, down to his very dog. Even his clothing is in danger. I saw it in his eyes. It is the disease which has pervaded his system. This new conscience of his won't let him do anything sensible."

"Judge Burnham," said Ruth, having endured all that she could — she was not skilled in endurance — "I wish you would remember that you are speaking of my father, and refrain from sneers. If his code of honor is higher than yours, he can not help it, I suppose. At least, you should be able to respect it; or, failing in that, please respect my feelings."

"I beg your pardon," said Judge Burnham, quickly startled by the repressed fierceness of the tones.

"I did not mean to hurt your feelings, Ruth. but you do not understand business, and your father is really being very absurd with his strained ideas of equity."

"I understand conscience, somewhat," Ruth said, quickly, and she was stung with the thought that perhaps in the days gone by she had stifled hers. Now all this was certainly very sad talk to come between husband and wife not six weeks after their marriage. Ruth felt it and deplored it and wept over it, and wondered how it would be possible to avoid subjects on which they did not think and feel alike.

Meantime she ought to go and see her father

From this she shrank. How could she talk with him from any other standpoint than that in which she had always known him? A man of wealth and power in the business world, she felt that he must be utterly bowed down. He had always, in a lofty, aristocratic way, attached full importance to wealth. How was he going to endure being suddenly thrown to the bottom of the ladder, when he had for so many years rested securely on the top round?

However, it was folly for her to avoid such an evident duty. She chose an hour when Mrs. Erskine would be undoubtedly engaged downstairs, and slipped away to the train, having said nothing of her intention to her husband when he went to town an hour before, and without having as yet succeeded in arranging a single sentence that she felt would be helpful to her father, she suddenly and silently presented herself before him, in the little room off the library which was sacred to his private use. He sat at the table, writing, his face pale, indeed, but quiet, not exactly cheerful, yet certainly peaceful.

He glanced up as the door opened, and then

arose quickly. "Well, daughter," he said, "you have come to see father in his trouble. That is right. Come in, dear, and have a seat." And with the old-time courtesy he drew an easy chair for her and waited while she seated herself. Then he sat down again, in his large arm-chair, before her.

"Yes," he said, "I must begin again. I shall not get to where I was before. On your account I regret it. I wanted to leave you a fortune to do good with, but your husband has enough, and it is all right. The Lord can choose what money he will have spent for him."

"You certainly need not think of me, father. As you say, Judge Burnham has enough." And even at this moment there was a pang in Ruth's heart that she would not have had her father see for worlds, as she wondered how much power she could have over *his* wealth to turn it into sources for good.

"My chief anxiety is, What are you going to do?"

"Well," he said, and there was a gleam of a smile on his face, "I am going to climb up again with my wife's help. It isn't poverty, you know, thanks to her. Isn't it marvelous how she can have saved so much out of the paltry yearly sums? Haven't you heard about it? Why, she actually has at interest about fourteen thousand dollars; invested in my name, too. Isn't that a reward for the indignities I heaped upon her?" His voice broke, and the tears started in his eyes. "I tell you," he said, tremulously, "I bore it all better than that. I knew I was not to blame for the financial downfall, but to find that the woman whom I had wronged had been all these years heaping coals of fire on my head just unmanned me," and he wiped the great tears from his cheeks, while Ruth moved restlessly in her seat. She did not like to hear about his having wronged "that woman," neither did she like to have her father beholden to *her* for support.

"It is fortunate that she saved it," she said, and her voice was most unsympathetic. "But, after all, father, it is your money."

"No, daughter, no; not a penny of it. Ten times that sum ought to belong to her. Think of trying to make *money* repair the injury which I was doing her! But it is most comforting to feel that I am to be beholden to her, rather than to any other human being."

Ruth did not think so.

"I have been wonderfully sustained, Ruth," her father continued. "I said last night that it was almost worth losing a fortune to see how calmly the Lord Jesus could hold me. I haven't had a doubt nor an anxiety as to its being the right way from the first hour that I knew of the loss. Of course I don't see *why* it should come, and really, I don't believe I care to know. Why should I, when I can so entirely trust to His wisdom and love? There is another thing, daughter — the sweet came with the bitter, and was so much more important that it overbalanced. Did you know that your mother had come into the sunlight of His love? She told me about it that very evening, and she says she owes her knowledge of the way to me. Isn't that a wonderful boon for the Lord to bestow on such as I?"

Ruth turned almost away from him, with an unaccountable irritability tugging at her heart. "Your mother!" he had never used those words to her before. They had slipped out now, un consciously. He had grown used to their sound in speaking to Susan; he did not see how they jarred. It frightened his daughter to realize how little she seemed to care whether a soul had been new-born or not; she could not take in its importance.

"I am sure I am very glad," she said, but her voice bore not the slightest trace of gladness. Then she went home, feeling that her spirit was not in accord with the tone of that house. "He doesn't need *my* comfort," she told herself, and she said it almost bitterly. It was true enough, he didn't. Not that he did not appreciate human sympathy and human love, but a greater than human strength had laid hold upon his weakness, and he was upborne. This, too, Ruth recognized, and even while she rejoiced in it, there mingled with the joy a strange pain.

Following the money downfall came plans that were quite in accord with her wishes. They sprang into being apparently through a chance remark. It began with Ruth, in a heavy sigh, as she said, she and Susan being alone:

"I don't know how to take the next step for those girls. It is absurd to think of sending them to school. At their age, and with their limited knowledge, they would be simply objects of ridicule. We must find a resident governess for them. But where to look for one who will have to teach young ladies what, in these days, quite little children are supposed to know, and yet remember that they are young ladies, and treat them as such, is a puzzle. I am sure I don't know where to look, nor how to describe what we need, the circumstances are so peculiar."

Then she waited for Susan to answer; and so accustomed had she grown to being helped by that young lady's suggestions, that she waited hopefully, though without having the least conception of how a comparative stranger in the city could help in this emergency.

"There are plenty to get," Susan said. "At least I suppose the world is full of teachers, if you only knew just where to look for them."

"Oh, *teachers*. Yes, there are plenty of them, if a teacher was all that was needed. But, you know, Susan, the case is a very unusual one. We really need a woman who knows a good deal about every thing, and who is as wise as a serpent. There is a chance to ruin the girls, and make trouble for Judge Burnham and misery for me, if we do not get just the right sort of person; and I am in doubt as to whether there *is* any right sort to be had."

Whereupon Susan laughed, and blushed a little, as she said:

"After such an alarming statement of the requirements, I am not sure that I have the courage to propose a friend of mine. She doesn't lay claim to any of the gifts which you suggest."

Ruth looked up, relieved and smiling.

"Do you really know a teacher, Susan, whom you can recommend? I forgot that your acquaintance was extensive among scholars. You need not hesitate to suggest, for I assure you that your recommendation would go further with Judge Burnham and myself than any one we know, for you understand the situation, and your judgment is to be relied upon. Of whom are you thinking, and where is she to be found? I can almost promise her a situation."

Whereupon Susan laughed outright.

"Really," she said, "you make it very embarrassing work for me. I not only have to recommend myself, but actually force myself upon your observation. But, since I intend to teach in the future, as I have done in the past, why not try me for awhile, since I am here? I think I would do until the girls were ready for somebody who could do better."

If she had been watching her sister's face she would have seen the puzzled look change to one of radiant delight. Then that sister did what, to one of her undemonstrative nature, was a strange thing to do — she crossed to Susan's side, and bending down, kissed her eagerly on either cheek.

"I believe I am an idiot!" she said. "Though I used to think I was capable of planning as well as most persons, but I never once thought of it! And I knew you meant to teach, too. It is the very thing. Nothing could be more delightful! Judge Burnham will think so, too. Oh, Susan, you are one of my greatest comforts!"

CHAPTER XXVI.

"THESE BE THY GODS."

AT last in Ruth Burnham's home, life settled into routine. Everything was as she had planned it. She had tried two ways of life. For a season almost everything had gone contrary to her desires and plans. Then there came this period wherein she was permitted to carry out, in detail, all the schemes which seemed to her wise. In the earlier days of her Christian experience she had felt, if she did not say, that if she could but have the control of her own affairs, humanly speaking, she could make things work together in a different and more helpful manner for herself and her friends.

It was as if the Lord had taken her at her word and opened the door for her to plan and carry out according to her will. The question was, Did she find it a success? Was she now, at last, a happy, growing Christian — one whose influence was felt in all the departments of her life? Oh, I am afraid that Ruth hated to admit, even to her own heart, how far from success she felt! Painful though the admission was, she had to make it to her conscience that she was neither a growing nor a happy Christian.

What was the trouble? Why, in her heart and in her life there was conflict. She knew the right, and too often she did it not. Give me such an experience as that, and you may be sure that you have given the record of an unhappy and an unfruitful life. There were so many ways in which Ruth could see that she had erred. She meant to commence in just the right way; she had taken great credit to herself for her sacrifice of personal ease and pleasure, for the taking up of hard crosses in connection with Judge Burnham's duties; yet now she saw that there were crosses far more important which she had not taken up at all.

Almost as often as she knelt alone in her own room to pray she knelt in tears. First, because she was always alone; her husband never bowed with her, never read the Bible with her. Was this, in part, her fault? What if, in those first days when everything was new, and when he was on the alert to be her comfort, she had asked him to read with her, to kneel with her, and hear her pray? Was it not possible that he might have done so? Well, those first days were not so long gone by. Was it not just possible that he might join her now?

Alas for Ruth! Though the days of her married life had been so few, she could look back upon them and see inconsistencies in word and manner and action which went far toward sealing her lips. Not that they should, but is it not the painful experience of each one of us that they so often do? If Ruth had but commenced right! It is so hard to make a beginning, in the middle of a life. Besides, there had been many words spoken by Judge Burnham which would serve to make it harder for him to yield to any innovations. If she had but beguiled him before these words were spoken! Then, indeed, it is possible that some of them at least would never have been uttered. Only a few weeks a wife, and for how many of her husband's sins was she already in a measure responsible?

Then the girls were a source of pain to Ruth's conscience. Not that they had not learned well her first lessons. It surprised, at times it almost alarmed her, to see with what eagerness they caught at the ribbons and ruffles, and all the outside adornments of life. They were entirely willing to give these, each and all, important place in their thoughts. She had given them intoxicating glimpses of the world of fashion before their heads or hearts were poised enough not to be over-balanced. They had caught at the glimpse and made a fairyland of beauty out of it, and had resolved with all their young, strong might to "belong" to that fairyland, and they looked up to and reverenced Ruth as the queen who had the power of opening these enchanted doors to them. You are to remember that, though backward, they were by no means brainless. Having been kept in such marked seclusion all their lives, until this sudden opening of the outer doors upon them, and this sudden flinging them into the very midst of the whirl of "what to wear and how to make it," hearing little else during these first bewildering days than the questions concerning this shade and that tint, and the comparative merits of ruffles or plaits, and the comparative qualities of silks and velvets, and the absolute necessity of perfect fitting boots and gloves and hats, what wonder that they jumped to the conclusion that these things were the marks of power in the world, and were second in importance to nothing?

Having plunged into her work with the same energy which characterized all Ruth's movements, how was she now to teach the lesson that these things were absolutely as nothings compared with a hundred other questions having to do with their lives?

She worked at this problem, and saw no more how to do it than she saw how to take back the first few weeks of married life and personal influence over her husband and live them over again. There was no solace in trying to talk her difficulties over with Susan, because she, while intensely sympathetic in regard to every-day matters, was gravely silent when Ruth wondered why the girls were so suddenly absorbed in the trivialities of life to the exclusion of more important things. And Ruth felt that her sister recognized *her* share in the matter and deplored it.

About her husband she chose to be entirely silent herself. If pride had not kept her so, the sense of wifely vows would have sealed her lips. At least she had high and sacred ideas of marriage vows. Alas for Ruth, there were other disquieting elements. She realized her husband's influence on herself. Try as she would, resolve as she might, steadily she slipped away from her former moorings. Little things, so called, were the occasions of the lapses, but they were not little in their effect on her spiritual life.

"How is it possible that you can desire to go to that stuffy little room and meet a dozen illiterate men and women or, is it a mistaken sense of duty which impels you?"

This was her husband's question regarding the suggestion of Ruth that they go to the weekly prayer-meeting. His tone was not unkind, but there was just a touch of raillery in it, which was at all times harder for Ruth to bear than positive coldness.

"You must be content to tolerate my tastes," she said, "since you can not sympathize with them. Endurance is the most that I can expect."

He laughed good-naturedly.

"Now, Ruth, dear, don't be cross. I haven't the least idea of being so, and I propose to humor your whims to the last degree. I will even escort you to that most uninviting room and call for you again, enduring, meantime, with what grace I can the sorrows of my country solitude. What more can you expect? But in return for such magnanimity you might enlighten my curiosity. Why do you go? How can I help being curious? In town, now, it was different. While I might even there question your choice of entertainments, at least you met people of culture, with whom you had certain ideas in common. But really and truly, my dear wife, I am at home in this region of country, so far as knowledge of the mental caliber of the people is concerned, and I assure you you will look in vain for a man or woman of

brains. Outside of the minister — who is well
enough, I suppose, though he is a perfect bore
to me — there is a general and most alarming
paucity of ideas. Besides which, there is no
gas in the church, you know, and kerosene
lamps are fearful at their best, and these, I
judge, are at their worst. So, taking the subject
in all its bearings, I think I am justified in asking what can be your motive?"

Is it any wonder that there were tears in
Ruth's eyes, as she turned them toward her husband? How explain to one who would not understand the meaning of her terms why she
sought the little country prayer-meeting?

"Judge Burnham," she said, speaking slowly,
and trying to choose the words with care, "is it
unknown to you that I profess to expect to meet
there with the Lord Jesus Christ?"

"Oh, that indeed!" he said, and the lightness
of his tone so jarred on her that she shivered.
"I believe that is an article in your creed. I
don't discredit it in its intellectual and spiritual
sense, but what does it prove? I suppose you
meet him equally in this room, and I suppose the
surroundings of this room are as conducive to

communion with the Unseen Presence as are those of that forlorn little square box of a church Isn't that the most doleful building for a church that it was ever your misery to see? It is abominably ventilated; for that matter churches nearly always are. I wonder if there is any thing in church creeds that conscientiously holds people from observing the laws of health and comfort? I don't believe there is an opera-house in the United States that would be tolerated for a season, if the question of light and heat and ventilation had been ignored in it as entirely as they are in churches."

What was there to be said to such as he? Perhaps Ruth said the best thing under the circumstances. "Well, come, don't let us discuss the subject further; there is the bell; please take me down to the poor little church, for I really want to go."

"Certainly," he said, rising promptly, and making ready with a good-natured air. He attended her to the very door and was on its threshold in waiting when the hour of prayer was over, and was gracious and attentive in the extreme during the rest of the evening, making no allusion to the prayer-meeting, after the first few mischievous and pointed questions as to the exercises, questions which tried Ruth's nerves to the utmost, for the reason that the little meeting had been so utterly devoid of anything like life and earnestness that it was a trial rather than a help to her.

Conversations not unlike these were common on prayer-meeting evening, always conducted on Judge Burnham's part, in the most gracious spirit, ending by accompanying her to the church door. She ceased to ask him to enter, for the reason that she was not sure but it would be a positive injury to him to do so. One Wednesday evening he followed her to the parlor with a petition :

"Now, wifie, I have been most patiently good every 'meeting' evening, since I had you all to myself, having given you up, if not willingly, at least uncomplainingly, to the companionship of those who are neither elevating nor inspiring. Now it is your turn to show yourself unselfish. I'm a victim to one of my old-fashioned headaches, to-night, and want you to take care of me."

To which proposition Ruth instantly agreed — the pang of conscience which she felt being not on account of the wife's obvious duty to care for a sick husband, but because of the instant throb of relief of which she was conscious in having a legitimate reason for escaping the prayer-meeting. It was too painfully apparent, even to her own heart, that she had not enjoyed the hour of religious communion; that she had sighed inwardly when the door closed after her retreating husband, and she had gone back eagerly to his companionship, directly after the hour of separation was over. It transpired that, on this occasion, his headache was not so severe, but that it admitted of his being entertained by his wife's voice reading aloud, and he was presently so far recovered as to sit up and join in her reading, giving her a lesson in the true rendering of Shakespeare, which was most enjoyable to both. On the following Wednesday there was a concert of unusual interest in the city, and Ruth obeyed her husband's summons by telegraph to come down on the six o'clock train and attend. Of course it would not do to have him wait in the city for her and disappoint him. Another Wednesday,

and she went again to the little meeting; but it
had in the interim grown more distasteful to her;
and, indeed, there was this excuse for poor Ruth,
that the meeting was one of the dullest of its
kind; there were no outside influences helping her.
It was a matter of hard duty between her and
her conscience. Perhaps when we consider that
human nature is what it is, we should not think
it strange that six weeks after the concert found
Ruth accepting an invitation to a select party in
town, forgetting utterly, until, in her estimation,
the acceptance was beyond recall, that it was Wednesday
evening. When she remembered it, she told
her long-suffering conscience somewhat roughly,
that "wives certainly had duties which they
owed to their husbands." I have given you now
only a specimen out of many influences which
slowly and surely drew Ruth down stream.
Susan, looking on, feeling for the present powerless,
except as that ever-present resource — prayer
— was left her, felt oftener perhaps than any
other command, the force of that one sentence:
"Thou shall have no other gods *before me*."

Yet was not Ruth Burnham happy. Perhaps
she had never, in her most discontented hours,

been further from happiness. Her conscience was too enlightened, and had, in the last two years, been too well cultivated for her not to know that she was going contrary very often to her former ideas of right.

Too surely she felt that her husband's views, her husband's tastes, her husband's plans of life were at variance with hers. It was all very well to talk about his yielding, and being led; he could yield to the inevitable; and there is a way of appearing to yield, gracefully, too, which develops itself as only a master-stroke to the end that one may gain one's own way. This method Judge Burnham understood in all its details.

His wife early in their married life began to realize it. She began to understand that he was, in a quiet, persistent way, actually *jealous* of the demands which her religion made upon her time and heart. It was not that he deliberately meant to overthrow this power which held her; rather he sought in a patient way to undermine it. Perhaps if Ruth had realized this, she might have been more on her guard. But Satan had succeeded in blinding her eyes by that most specious of all reasonings that she must, by her concession to his tastes and plans, win him over to her ways of thinking. In other words, she must, by doing wrong, convince him of the beauty that there is in a consistent Christian life, and win him to the right way! In matters pertaining to this life Ruth's lip would have curled in scorn over such logic. Why was it that she could not see plainly the ground whereon she trod?

Is there, then, no rest in the Christian life? Is the promise, " Come unto me, and I will give you rest," utterly void and worthless? Has not God called his children to " peace? " Is there no " peace which passeth understanding," such as the world can neither give nor take away?

Why did not Ruth Burnham, with her educated mind and clear brain, ponder these things, and determine whether, when she told herself, that of course one must expect conflict and heart-wars in this life, she was not thereby making the eternal God false to his covenants?

What was the trouble? Why, the same thing which comes in so continually with its weary distractions — a divided heart. " Whosoever therefore will be a friend of the world is the enemy of God!" That old solemn truth remains to-day, after eighteen hundred years of experience, a *truth* which many a world-tossed soul has proved; and Ruth Burnham had need to learn that it matters not whether the world be represented by a general glitter, or by a loving husband, so that the object of special choice was placed "*before*" *Him*, solemn effect must follow.

CHAPTER XXVII.

THE BAPTISM OF SUFFERING.

IN the course of time it became to Susan Erskine, who was watching with eager interest the story of her sister's life, a question of painful moment as to how the watchful Christ would come to the rescue of his straying sheep. For, as the days passed, it grew most painfully apparent that Ruth *was* straying. She did not gain in the least. This being the case, it is of course equivalent to saying that she lost. Steadily her husband proved the fact that his was the stronger nature, and that he was leading, not being led. Yet his wife did not get entirely out of the way — not far enough out indeed, to claim the few pitiful returns that the world has for service. She staid always in that wretched middle state, not belonging to the world fully, nor yet fully to Christ; hence, continuous soreness of heart, developing alternately in gloom and irritability.

There came at last a messenger to her home and heart — a little, tender, helpless one, just helpless enough and clinging enough to gather all the tendrils of the heart around and bind them closely. How that baby was loved! There have been babies loved before — many a heart has bowed before the shrine of such an idol; but perhaps never baby, from grandfather down to the little hired nurse, whose duty it was in the course of time to keep said baby amused, had such patient, persistent, willing slaves as had this young heir of the house of Burnham. As for Ruth, she found that she had never even *dreamed* of the depth of mother-love. A sort of general interest in healthy, cleanly, well-dressed children had been one of her pastimes. She had imagined herself somewhat fond of certain types of childhood, while aware that she shrank in horror from certain other types. But this new, strange rush of emotions which filled her heart almost to bursting was an experience of which she had had no conception. From that hour those who watched Ruth anxiously to see whether the sweet young life which was a part of herself would win her back to her covenant vows, saw with ever-deepening pain that this new-born soul was only another and a stronger idol. With all the fierceness of her strong nature, with all the unrest of her dissatisfied heart, did the mother bow before this tiny soul and bring it worship. She discovered at last that self-sacrifice was easy; that sleepless nights, and restless days, and the pressure of many cares and responsibilities were as nothing, provided baby's comfort demanded any or all of these.

Now she withdrew entirely from the prayer-meetings, and ceased her fitful attempts at being identified with the Sabbath-school. She was even most rare in her attendance on the regular Sabbath service. Did not baby require a mother's care? This was her trust — God-given surely, if anything ever was — and therefore she was to consider it as a work from him.

There is no error so fatal as a *half* truth. To

be sure, this theory was not carried out in all respects. The mother found time for social life. She was seen frequently at concerts and lectures, and entertainments of various sorts, but this, she said, was a duty she owed to her husband. And it really seemed as though there were no voice left in her heart to remind her that the duties she owed to Christ were being neglected. And Susan, watching and waiting, began to ask her heart half fearfully, "How will he speak to her next?" That he *would* speak to her, and that effectually, she fully believed, for Ruth was surely one of his own. How strange that she *would* wander and make it necessary for the Shepherd to seek her with bleeding feet, "over the mountains, wild and bare," instead of resting securely and sweetly within the fold!

Meantime the domestic machinery of the Burnham household worked more smoothly than it is always wont to do under the peculiar family relations.

Ruth, whatever her faults, was fully alive to the special cause of comfort in her household. She never ceased to realize that one of the greatest blessings of her lot in life was the sud den descent upon her of a sister. Such a faithful, thoughtful, self-sacrificing sister!—one who really seemed to be as "wise as a serpent, and as harmless as a dove." Even Ruth, though she had an idea that she fully appreciated her, did not see the extent of her influence over those untutored girls. Daily her power over them increased; the development in them mentally was something of which their father was unceasingly proud; not the less, perhaps, did it give him satisfaction because there was coupled with it a development of refinement of tone and manner, a growing sense of the fitness of things, and an evident and hearty relish for the advantages which his wealth was able to afford them.

Over one thing Susan pondered and prayed, and watched with no little anxiety: the girls were willing to be her pupils in any other study save that of personal religion; they were in a degree interested in Bible study; they by no means shrank from it; they respected her views, they talked freely with her as to creeds and doctrines; but when it came to pressing their personal need of Christ as a Saviour from sin, they were strangely apathetic.

"Had they inherited their father's distaste for all the personalities of religion?" Susan questioned, "or had their first delicious glimpse of this new world, given under the new mother's tutelage, so stamped their ambitions that they had no room for deeper thoughts?" From this last solution she shrank; it made such an awfully solemn matter of personal responsibility; yet when she saw the almost reverence in which they held this new mother's views of whatever pertained to outside life, she could not but feel that there had been stamped upon their hearts the belief that she who had reigned so long in the fashionable world knew all about the important things, and *had shown them what they were!* At least, Susan felt sure that, could Ruth have realized the influences she possessed over the unformed minds of her two daughters, she would have shrunken from using it for trivialities.

As for Ruth, the girls had become secondary matters to her. She had carried her point; she had proved that dress and attention to the many refinements of life would make a vast difference in these two; she had shown their father that it was through sheer neglect that they grew to be the painful trials which they were; she had proved to him that her course was the right one. There was no skeleton in their country home now, to be avoided painfully. The girls were not perfect in deportment, it is true; but so rapid had been their advancement in certain ways, and so skillful was the brain which planned their outward adornings, that they might safely endure introductions as Judge Burnham's daughters, in any circle where it was desirable to present them. Ruth felt, watching them, that even the famous criminal lawyer himself would never have recognized in them the two distressing specimens which he had characterized as "discarded American help." She had shown her husband, also, that country life was not only endurable, but, in many respects, desirable; indeed, so satisfied had he become with his lovely rural home, that, when it was announced as important for baby's health that the entire season should be spent there, he offered no objection, and agreed with alacrity to Ruth's plan that Susan should take the girls for a peep at life at Long Branch, and leave them to the solitude of home. "Very well," he had said, "provided you will, on their return, leave Susan in charge of his lordship, and run away with me to the mountains for a few days." And Ruth had laughed, and shrugged her handsome shoulders, and exclaimed over the folly of trying to coax a mother from her six-months-old baby, for any mountains in the world; and then she had looked proudly over toward the lace-curtained crib, and rejoiced in the fact that the hero sleeping there had power enough to hold father as well as mother a meek worshipper at his shrine; for, if Judge Burnham really *was* an idolater, his only son was the supreme idol in his inmost heart.

So the summer plans were carried out. Ruth serenely discussed seaside outfits, and decided, with the tone of one who realized that her word was law, as to whether Minta would look better in a salmon-colored evening dress, and whether Seraph was too young for a satin-trimmed one. Long ago Susan, apparently without thought on the subject, had started the habit of softening the objectional name into this euphonious one; and Ruth remarked to her husband that perhaps time would develop the fact that there was a most a prophecy in the name, if Sereph's **voice** continued to develop in strength and sweetness, under culture. On the whole, there was serene satisfaction in the survey of her handiwork where these girls were concerned; they bade fair to do justice to her discernment, and afford food for pride. Still, as I said, they were secondary. So that they were always well dressed, and sat properly at table, and entered a room properly, and bowed gracefully to her callers, and treated her with unfailing respect, she was at rest concerning them. *Almost*, she had so trodden her conscience under foot that in these days had she really very little trouble in the thought that her *best* for them had ignored the *best* which life had for any soul.

Susan packed, and arranged, and listened to her numerous directions, and went off to take her first summering away from cares, which of one sort or another had held her for a lifetime — went with a shade of anxiety on her face which was not for herself, nor yet because of her responsibility in regard to these two unfledged worldlings, but for the Christian mother hovering over the lace-curtained crib in the rose-hued nursery;

and her heart went murmuring, "How will He speak to her next?"

Not many days after, the next call of the Shepherd came. You are prepared to hear what it was — that little, sheltered, watched-over baby fell sick; not very sick; not so but that the doctor went and came with a cheery air, and told the anxious mother that they would have her darling as chirk as ever in a day or two, and Judge Burnham believed him, and laughed at the mother's dreary face, and made light of her fears; but poor Ruth did *not* believe him, and went about her mother cares and hung over her sick darling with an ever-increasing, deadening weight at her heart. He was not the family physician of the Erskines — Dr. Mitchell — Judge Burnham didn't believe in *him*, so the coming and going doctor was the one associated with the dark days wherein they had waited and watched over Ruth's father.

Whether it was that association, or whatever it was, Ruth shrank a little from Dr. Bacon, and was not able to give him her full confidence. Dark days were these, and they dragged their slow lengths along, and brought regularly the longer and darker nights, for it is at night that we hang most hopelessly over our sick, and the silence and quietness of the home grew oppresive to Ruth. She wished for Susan, she would gladly have had the girls coming and going, yet it seemed foolish to send for them; there was a skillful nurse, and there were neighbors, who, though they had been almost ignored by the fine family at the Hill, yet directly they heard that there was sickness, came and went with their thoughtful offers of assistence. Why, even Mrs. Ferris, with her loud voice and her uncouth ways, came and was welcomed by Ruth, because of the humble work which she did in the kitchen that tended to baby's comfort.

And still the doctor came and went with his story that the baby would be all right in a few days; but the days of mending did not come, and the shadow deepened and darkened, though as yet it seemed to be seen only by the mother's heart, and in that heart a war was being waged which in fierceness and length of conflict so far transcended all Ruth's other struggles with life as to make them pale into nothingness before her. And the struggle was such that no human heart could intermeddle, for it was between Ruth and God! She realized in those days that she had actually had many a struggle with the great God before, without recognizing it as such, or at least calling it by its right name.

At first there was wild, fierce rebellion; she clung to her baby, held him, indeed, so fiercely that he wailed feebly, and looked up into her face almost in terror, and she cried out that she could not — indeed, *would not* — give him up; no, not even to the Giver! And the little face grew daily more wasted, and the little hands more feeble, and the moments of wakeful recognition shorter, and the hours of half stupor longer, and the doctor grew less cheery when he came, and Judge Burnham grew restless and nervous — went later every day to town and returned earlier, and was, in his silent, restrained, yet passionate way, fully as rebellious as his wife.

CHAPTER XXVIII.

"THE OIL OF JOY."

EVEN yet the doctor had said no word of discouragement. And Judge Burnham had, though he had ceased laughing at Ruth fears, sharply controverted them. And she? — she felt she would have stricken down any one who had breathed a word of danger. It was fearful enough to feel it; let no one dare to *speak* it. Once when Judge Burnham — filled with pity for her loneliness during the hours when he was obliged to be away — suggested recalling the travellers, she turned toward him fiercely:

"Why?" she asked him; "what do you mean? Are you keeping something from me?

Does the Doctor tell you what he does not me? Judge Burnham, I will never forgive you if you deceive me."

"Why, no," he said, "Ruth, no; why will you be so unreasonable? The Doctor says he sees no ground as yet for special anxiety. He says to me just what he says to you. No one thinks of deception. I only felt that it would be less lonely with the girls at home; and Susan would be a comfort."

"Comfort!" she said, still speaking sharply. "Why have I need of comfort? I have my baby, and I can take care of him; and as for loneliness, the house is full from morning till night. One would think people never heard of a sick child before. They are always sick when teething. Why should we be so unreasonably frightened?"

And Judge Burnham turned away sighing, patient with his wife, for he saw that she was too wildly frightened to talk or act like a reasonable being.

Among all the comers and goers there was one who did not come. That was Mrs. Judge Erskine. Not that she would not have willingly been there both day and night; but poor Ruth, who had never recovered in the least from her early discomfort concerning the woman, in this time of her frenzy felt the dislike increasing to almost hatred. She tortured herself at times with imagining the exclamations that the odious grandmother would make over the change in her darling, until at last it grew to be almost an insanity to her; and she fiercely ordered that no word of any sort should be taken to her home. "Father shall not be needlessly troubled," was outward reason enough, for Judge Erskine was not strong this season; so, beyond the knowledge that the child was not very well, was teething, and kept Ruth closely at home, the two people left in the old Erskine homestead together knew nothing.

Slowly yet surely, the Shepherd was reaching after his stray sheep. By degrees her mood and her prayers changed; they lost their fierceness, but not one whit of their will-power. She began to feel herself in the hands of God. She gave up her defiance, and came to him as a suppliant. She sat alone in the shadows of a long night of watching, and looked over her life, and saw plainly her mistakes, her wanderings, her sins

Then she fell on her knees beside that crib, one watching eye and listening ear intent on every change of expression or breathing in the darling, and then and there she proceeded to make terms with God. If he would only give her back her darling, her boy, she would live, oh *such* a different life! — a life of entire consecration. All she had, and was, and hoped to be, her husband, her baby — everything should be consecrated, be held second to his love. Long she knelt there praying, but no answering voice spoke peace to her heart. And the struggle, though changed in its form, went on and on by degrees, and Ruth with her long preoccupied heart was very slow to learn the lesson. She was made to understand that God had never promised to compromise with his own, never promised to hear a prayer which began with an "if." Entire consecration meant all the ifs thrown down at the feet of the Lord, for him to control as he would. Solemnly his voice spoke to her heart, spoke as plainly as though the sound of it had echoed in the silent room: "And *if* I take your darling into my arms of infinite love, and shield him for you in heaven, what then?" And Ruth realized with a shudder that then, her heart said it would only be infinite mercy that could keep her from hating God! But when she realized this solemn, this *awful* truth, which proved rebellion in the heart that had long professed allegiance, God be thanked that she did not get up from her kneeling and go away again with the burden. She knelt still, and, with the solemn light of the All-seeing Eye flashing down into her soul, she confessed it all — her rebellion, her selfish determination to hold her treasure whether God would or not, her selfish desire to compromise, her cowardly, pitiful subterfuge of promising him that which was already his by right, *if* he would submit to her plans. The long, sad, sinful story was laid bare before him, and then her torn heart said: "Oh, Christ, I can not help it; I hold to my darling, and I *can not* give him up, even when I would. Oh, thou Saviour of human souls, even in their sinfulness, what shall I do?" Did ever such heart-cry go up to the Saviour of souls in vain?

You do not need me to tell you that before the dawn of the coming morning filled the room a voice of power had spoken peace. The plans, and the subterfuges, and the rebellings, and the "ifs,' all were gone. "As thou wilt," was the only voice left in that thoroughly bared and bleeding heart.

It was even then that the shadow fell the darkest. When the doctor came next morning, for the first time he shook his head.

"Things do not look so hopeful as they did, here," he said.

And Judge Burnham, turning quickly toward his wife, looking to see her faint or lose her reason (he hardly knew which phase of despair to expect), saw the pale, changed face.

"Is there no hope, Doctor?" and her voice though low, was certainly calmer than it had been for days.

"Well," said the Doctor, relieved at her method of receiving his warning, "I never like to say that. While there is life there is hope, you know; but the fact is, I am disappointed in the turn that the trouble has taken. I am a good deal afraid of results."

Had Ruth spoken her thoughts, she would have said: "I have been awfully afraid of results for a week; but a voice of greater power than yours has spoken to me now. It rests with Him, not you; and I think he wants my darling." What she *did* say was:

"Ought the girls to be summoned?"

"Well," said Dr. Bacon, regarding her curiously, "if it is important that they should be here, I think I should telegraph."

Then, presuming upon long acquaintance with Judge Burnham, he said, as they passed down the hall together:

"Upon my word, Burnham, you have the most unaccountable wife in the world."

"Comments are unnecessary, Doctor," Judge Burnham said, in his haughtiest tones, and the next instant the front door closed with a bang, and the father had shut himself and his pain into the little room at the end of the hall. What was *he* to do? which way turn? how live? He had never until this moment had other than a passing anxiety. Now the whole crushing weight of the coming blow seemed to fall on him, and he had not the force of habit, nor the knowledge of past experiences, to drive him to his knees for a refuge. Instead, his fierce heart raved. If Ruth had been in danger of hating God, he felt, yes, actually realized, that his heart was filled at this moment with a fierce and bitter hatred. Can you imagine what the trials of that day were to Ruth? Have you any knowledge of what a shock it is to a torn and bleeding heart, which yet feels that the Almighty Father, the Everlasting Saviour, holds her and her treasure in the hollow of his hand, to come in contact with one who fiercely, blasphemously tramples on that trust? In this moment of supreme pain, it was given to Ruth's conscience to remember that she had chosen for her closest friend one who made no profession of loyalty to her Redeemer — the *Lover* of her child. Why should she expect to rest on him now?

This day, like all the other dark ones, drew toward its closing; the Doctor watched and waited for, and dispatched for, did not come, and the night drew about them; and it so happened that, save the nurse and the household servants, the father and mother were alone with their baby. Early in the afternoon, a sudden remembrance had come to Ruth, and she had turned from the crib long enough to say. "Let father know." And the messenger had gone, but even from him there was no response.

So they watched and waited. Judge Burnham, in feverish madness of anxiety, paced the floor, and alternately raged at the absent Doctor for not coming, and then wished he might never look upon his face again. Ruth staid on her knees beside that crib, from which for hours she had not moved, and her lips continually formed that inaudible prayer, "Thy will be done." And really and truly the awful bitterness of the agony was gone out of her heart. There was a sound of wheels crunching the graveled drive — a bustle outside; somebody had come. Ruth glanced up, half fearfully. What was coming to break the solemn holiness of the hour? Not the Doctor, surely, with such bustle of noise. The door opened quickly, and they pressed in — her father, a tall stranger just beside him, and Mrs. Judge Erskine! *She* pushed past them both.

"Dear heart," she said, bending down to the crib, but her words were for Ruth, not the baby. "We just got the word. I brought Dr. Parmelee; I couldn't help it, child; I've seen him do such wonderful things. Your pa don t believe in his medicines — little bits of pills, you know — and he said your husband didn't but, la! what difference does that make? Men never do. They believe in getting 'em well, though. Come here, Dr. Parmelee. His pulse is real strong, and he looks to me as though he might — "

And here Mrs. Erskine paused for breath. She had been, in the meantime, throwing off her wraps, touching the baby's hand with skillful fingers, touching the hot head, and rising at last to motion the Doctor forward — the tall stranger. He came hesitatingly, looking toward the father; but Judge Burnham caught at his name.

"Anything, Doctor — anything!" he said, hoarsely. Dr. Bacon has proved himself an idiot. It is too late now; but, in heaven's name, do something."

Did it ever occur to you as strange that such men as Judge Burnham, in their hours of great mental pain, are very apt to call for blessings in "heaven's name?"

It was a strange hour! Ruth, who had been hushed into silence and solemnity by the presence of the Death Angel, found herself whirled into the very midst of the struggle for life. Dr. Parmelee declared, with Mrs. Erskine, that there was still a good deal of strength, and he hoped. And then he stopped talking and went to work — quietly, skillfuly, without commotion of any sort, yet issuing his orders with such swiftness and skill that mother and nurse, especially the former, were set to work to *do* instead of think. Especially was Mrs. Erskine alert, seeming to know by a sort of instinct, such as is noticeable in nurses who have a special calling for their work, what the Doctor wanted done, and how to do it. Far into the night they obeyed and watched. At last the Doctor rose up from a careful examination of his little patient.

"I believe," he said, speaking quietly, "I believe there has been a change in the symptoms in the past two hours. If I mistake not, the crisis is past. I think your little one will recover."

At the sound of these words, Judge Burnham strode over from his station at the head of the crib, and, grasping the Doctor's hand, essayed to speak words, but his voice choked, and the self-possessed, polished gentleman lost every vestige of control, and broke into a passion of tears.

"He is in God's hands, my friend," the new Doctor said gently; "he will do right; and I think he has given the little life back to you."

As for Ruth, she turned one look away from her baby's face toward the Doctor's; and he said as he went out from the home: "I declare that woman's eyes paid me to-night."

There was little talk and much watching during the rest of the night and the day that followed. Mrs. Erskine kept her post, keeping up that sort of alert *doing* which the skillful nurse understands so well, and which thrills the heart of a watcher with eager hope. One of Judge Burnham's first morning duties was to send a curt and courteous note — if both terms are admissible — to Dr. Bacon, asking for his bill. Then his own carriage waited at the train for the coming of Dr. Parmelee.

"Now, look here, child," said Mrs. Erskine, as, toward the midnight of the following night, Ruth turned for a moment from the crib and pressed her hand to her eyes, "you are just to go to bed and get a night's sleep. We'll have *you* on our hands, if you don't, as sure as the world; and that will be a nice mess for baby, bless his heart. Judge Burnham, you just take her and put her to bed. I'm going to sit by my little boy, here, the whole blessed night; I won't even wink; and when I undertake to watch, why I *watch*, and know how, though I do say it that shouldn't."

So, through much protesting from Ruth, and overruling by her father and husband, she was carried off to the room adjoining. In the gray dawn of another morning, she, having slept for four hours the sleep of utter exhaustion, started with a sudden, affrighted waking, wherein all the agony of the past days flashed over her, and, without waiting to remember the after-scene of joy, rushed to her nursery. There was the little crib, with its sleeping treasure; there on the couch, lay the tired nurse, sleeping quietly; there, at the crib's side, sat Mrs. Erskine, keeping her faithful, tireless vigil. She looked up with a reassuring smile as Ruth came in.

"What did you wake up for? He's as nice as a robin in a nest of down. He breathes just as easy! and the skin feels moist and natural

See how his little hair curls with the dampness! Anybody can see with half an eye that he is a great deal better. He'll get on now real fast, Dr. Parmelee says so. I never did see the like of them little pills! Ain't bigger than pinheads, neither."

Ruth bent low over the crib. The bounding pulse was quiet and steady at last; the breath came in slow, soft respirations, with no horrible gratings; the beautiful little hand, resting on the pillow, was doubled up as in the grace in which he held it when in health. Suddenly there rushed over Ruth all the probabilities of that solemn night, and all the blessings of this hour. After she had given him up utterly to God; after she had said, "Though he slay me, yet will I trust;" after she had said, "I am thine forever, Lord, *entirely*, though with empty arms," then he had given her back her trust — offered her one more chance to train the soul for him. With the thought came also the remembrance of the door through which he had opened this blessed paradise of hope, and she turned suddenly, and, burying her head in Mrs. Erskine's ample lap, cried out: "Oh, mother

mother! God bless you forever!" And the first tears that her tired eyes had felt for a week fell thick and fast.

"Land alive!" said Mrs. Judge Erskine. "Poor, dear heart! You are all tuckered out! You just go right straight back to bed. I won't turn my eyes away from him, and he's all right anyhow. I know the signs. Bless your heart, I nursed Mrs. Stevens' baby only last week, and this very Dr. Parmelee was there; and I saw what them little pills and powders could do when the Lord chose to use 'em. You just go back, dearie, this minute. You can sleep all day as well as not. Grandma'll take care of her blessed little darling, so she will."

And Ruth went back to the bedside, and to her knees; and among the sentences of her prayer that morning was this, from a full heart:

"O God! I thank thee, that, despite all the blindness and rebellion of my heart, thou didst send to me a *mother*. Thou hast given me 'the oil of joy for mourning, and the garment of praise for the spirit of heaviness.'"

THE END.

www.ingramcontent.com/pod-product-compliance
Lightning Source LLC
Chambersburg PA
CBHW051728300426
44115CB00007B/506